Mary McGrigor grew up in a fifteenth-century Scottish castle, which inspired her love of history. Married at twenty to Sir Charles MacGrigor, she was firstly a soldier's wife before becoming much involved in farming and breeding Highland ponies on a hill farm in Argyll. The author of many books, largely on historical biographies, and contributions to magazines, she has her family of four children, twelve grandchildren and two little great granddaughters to keep her occupied, while still finding time to write.

To the memory of Lady Mary Stewart, world famous author and great friend.

Mary McGrigor

THE GREAT SURVIVOR

The Amazing Escapes of James VI of Scotland and I of England

AUSTIN MACAULEY PUBLISHERS™

LONDON • CAMBRIDGE • NEW YORK • SHARJAH

A CIP catalogue record for this title is available from the British Library.

ISBN 9781788782074 (Paperback)
ISBN 9781788782081 (Hardback)
ISBN 9781788782098 (E-Book)

www.austinmacauley.com

First Published (2018)
Austin Macauley Publishers Ltd
25 Canada Square
Canary Wharf
London
E14 5LQ

My thanks to all who have helped me with this book must include my ancestor, Sir Archibald Edmonstone, the family historian, for the story of the Laird of Drumquhassle, largely forgotten today. Also a very big thank you to Connor Browne and other members of the Austin Macauley Production team, for all their assistance and most professional advice.

CONTENTS

PART 1

CHAPTER 1
Edinburgh, April 1543

An ice-cold wind swept in from the North Sea making men shrink into their doublets and women their shawls. Nonetheless, it did not deter them from lining the streets and thronging the windows of the small town of Linlithgow on this day of early April 1543. "Who is he?" many of them were asking. "Why the soldiers? Is this the start of another war?"

The man they were all peering at rode on a well-caparisoned horse at the head of a party of armed men. That they were French could be gathered from their appearance; the all-encasing armour reaching down to the knees and the helmet with a steel flap covering the back of the neck. Also their conversation, the orders barked out by the sergeant-at-arms, left no one in any doubt that they were neither Scottish nor English and most probably French.

But it was not the soldiers who most entranced the spectators, pushing and shoving each other to get a better view, shovelling their freezing feet on the cobbles to try to get them warm. Instead, all eyes were fixed on the leader, astride what was plainly a pure-bred horse. A tall man, his auburn hair covered head by one of the large caps that were all the fashion at the time, his small beard well-trimmed, he wore a fur-lined cloak over the steel corselet that all men of noble birth habitually kept on for protection against lead bullets and assassins' knives.

Sparks flew from the great charger's iron-shod hooves as its rider spurred him on up the hill from the town of Linlithgow to the royal palace standing on an eminence overlooking a loch now lashed with wind-driven spray. Reaching the main gate, as he requested entrance, the portcullis rose to admit what was obviously an expected guest. Dismounting, he handed the reins to a waiting groom before entering the palace courtyard where the elaborate fountain, master-stroke of the additions made by the late King James V, was the ultimate perfection of the great five-storied building, thought to be one of the finest examples of architecture in Europe. Once within the palace, the visitor found pages waiting to conduct him to the royal apartments of the Queen Dowager, widow of King James V, herself a native of France, daughter of the Duc de Guise.

Mary of Guise, as she was known in Scotland, an exceptionally tall woman, almost the height of the man who now knelt before her in a deep obeisance, still wore the black robes of mourning for the husband who had died just over a year before. Bidding the noble, whom she knew him to be, to rise to his feet, she addressed him in French, first language for both of them as the dowager Queen well knew. How delightful it was to hear him answer so fluently in the same tongue, sounding like music to her ear. Mary of Guise felt her pulse race faster, as on straightening to his feet, his eyes met her own.

Matthew, Earl of Lennox, was a handsome man, whom the Queen recognised as such. But it was not only his presence that she welcomed, delightful as that was proving to be, but for news of the little Duc de Longueville, son from her first marriage to Louis II d'Orléans, whom she had been forced to leave behind when she had been remarried to the Scottish King.

It was only after Matthew Lennox had reassured her that little Francis was well that she asked him how and for what purpose he had come. He told her that King Francis had sent him specifically to strengthen the ties of the long-established alliance between France and Scotland against the avaricious designs of the English King Henry VIII.

Matthew himself, although born in Scotland, had been taken to France for safety after the cruel murder of his father, stabbed in the back by Hamilton of Finnart, illegitimate son of the Earl of Arran, habitual enemy of his family, after he had actually surrendered to him following the battle of Linlithgow Bridge in September 1526. Aged ten when this happened, Matthew had then been brought up in France by the French branch of the Stuart family, the Seigneurs d'Aubigny, who had established themselves in that country (Stewart becoming Stuart) as mercenary soldiers. Now, 18 years later, sailing from France, with a small convoy of ships, he had contrived to avoid the patrolling war-ships of the English and to land safely at Dumbarton, a royal castle since the time of King David I, which, standing to guard the entrance of the great river Clyde, lay within the lands of the Lennox, hereditary to Matthew's family since the inauguration of the earldom in the 12th century by King William the 'Lion'.

Matthew had been sent to Scotland by King Francis to try to win a promise for his son, the dauphin, for the hand of the little Queen Mary of Scotland, now some 16 months old. The French King, like most others in western Europe, knew through his spies that the King of England, Henry VIII, through the auspices of the Earl of Arran, regent for the little queen since the death of her father, James V, was already angling for a marriage between her and his son, the Prince of Wales, the future King Edward VI. It was because the Queen's mother, Mary of Guise, was so strongly opposed to this that the French King Francis was determined, at whatever the cost, to strengthen the bonds between Scotland and France. First formed by the 'Aulde Alliance', an agreement, dating from the treaty signed by John Balliol, when King of Scotland and Philip IV of France, against Edward I of England in 1295. It had lasted for nearly three hundred years.

The French King's choice of ambassador was, however, questionable, the enmity between the houses of Lennox and Hamilton being in France, as elsewhere in Europe, so well known.

The roots of the quarrel between them lay in rival claims to the line of succession to the Scottish throne. The heads of both families had descended from the daughters of King James II. James Hamilton, 2nd Earl of Arran, was the great-grandson of the elder daughter, but there was some doubt of his legitimacy due to his father's, the 1st Earl's divorce: his first wife being still alive, although claimed to be an invalid, when he had married the mother of his heir. Lennox, although descended from the King's younger daughter, had thus, in the eyes of his partisans, a better claim than Arran to succeed, should the little Queen die childless, to what would then be a vacant throne.

Such was the discordancy between the rival parties in Scotland that it was even suggested that Matthew, despite the age gap of quarter of a century, should himself be betrothed to the one-year-old queen. There was more sense, and indeed more probability, in the idea that he should instead marry her mother, the Dowager Queen. Matthew, greatly attracted to her as he appears to have been, might well have adhered to this suggestion, but Mary of Guise, strong-minded and sensible, refused to agree. Twice widowed already, she wanted only to see her daughter become queen of the country of her birth.

Prior to the visit of Lennox with offers of a French marriage for the Scottish Queen, James Hamilton, the 2nd Earl of Arran, chosen by the Scottish councillors to rule as regent during the little queen's minority, at that time a Protestant, had arranged her betrothal to the son of the English king, Henry VIII. The Treaties of Greenwich had been signed on 1 July 1543. By their terms, it had been arranged that the marriage of Mary, Queen of Scots, to Edward, Prince of Wales, should be performed by proxy when the Queen reached the age of ten, at which time she was to leave for England[1]. King Henry, delighted, had even thrown in a bribe to the regent of his daughter, Princess Elizabeth, as a bride for Arran's son, the Master of Hamilton. He had promised him then that if he met resistance to the proposed marriages, he would send an army of 5,000 men to reinforce him. Also, if the 'French Party' in Scotland arranged another marriage for their queen, he would personally see to it that Arran became King of Scotland beyond the Forth.

Henry had then sent Sir Ralph Sadler, as his ambassador, to ensure that his wishes were enforced. But Sadler, after only two days in Edinburgh, had realised that the English King's insistence on having custody of the Scottish Queen would be so unpopular in Scotland that the regent, who was renowned for his inconsistency, would desert to the French allegiance. His foresight proved correct. Within days of ratifying the agreement with England, Arran had capitulated to the French/Catholic faction in Scotland and on 11 December, the Scottish Parliament had denounced the treaties with England and confirmed those made with France.

In the meanwhile, Mary of Guise, the Queen mother, had ensured the safety of her daughter by taking her to Stirling Castle, most secure fortress in Scotland, from where it was less likely that agents of Henry VIII could carry her off to England as she knew was planned. It was at the Royal Chapel in Stirling Castle that the little Mary was crowned Queen of Scotland on 9

September 1543. Matthew, Earl of Lennox, was in attendance, but spurned by the Queen Mother, he now saw the advantages of adhering to the English cause. Nonetheless at Dumbarton, he took charge of the munitions and money, brought by the French envoys, without revealing the change of allegiance he had made.

But Lennox was not amongst them. He had escaped to the safety of his own great fortress of Dumbarton Castle, crouching like a predator ready to pounce on hostile shipping at the entrance to the Clyde, from where, two months later, he sailed by night through the Irish Sea, down the south-west coast of Scotland and on to England where he came ashore at Chester before making his way overland to Carlisle.

There, by arrangement, he met King Henry's delegate Lord Wharton, deputy-warden of the English marches, who dictated King Henry's terms. Matthew must give his promise to hand over not only Dumbarton Castle but the other royal castle of Rothesay as well. Furthermore he must agree to do everything in his power to prevent the young Queen Mary being sent to France. Instead, he would carry her over the border to the English King. This being accomplished, Henry, for his part, guaranteed to make Matthew Lord Governor of Scotland while offering him the hand of his niece, the Lady Margaret Douglas, daughter of Henry's sister Queen Margaret of Scotland by her second marriage to the Earl of Angus, together with a yearly pension of 500 English marks.

Lennox, with these tempting prospects set before him, finally decided to accept the English King's offer and forsake his loyalty to France. Leaving his brother Robert, the designate Bishop of Orkney, as a hostage in return for his commitment. He returned to his ship at Chester and made full sail for London and the Thames.

Matthew Lennox, who had reached London by 26 June 1544, having sworn allegiance to Henry, was then offered the hand of the Lady Margaret Douglas, daughter of James IV's widow Queen Margaret by her second unhappy marriage to Archibald Douglas, Earl of Angus, together with the promised yearly pension of 500 English marks. On 6 July 1544, the couple were married in the chapel of St James's Palace.

They made a handsome pair, as even the critical George Buchanan, biographer of the great Scottish reformer John Knox, averred. Praising Margaret for her beauty and comeliness of person, he called Matthew, "one of the most admired cavaliers in France." King Henry himself dictated the letters of nationalisation for both Lennox and his secretary, a man called Tom Bishop and later, at the banquet following the wedding, declared that, in the event of his own children failing to follow him, he would be "right glad if heirs of Margaret's body succeeded to the crown."[2]

Matthew, as a vassal of King Henry, then formally surrendered to him the forfeited royal castles of Rothesay and Dumbarton, while Henry, in return, gave him property in England; consisting of the lands of Temple Newsam, near Leeds, recently forfeited from Lord D'Arcy and Meynell, one of the leaders of the rising of the Catholic lords of the north of England against Henry VIII's assumption of the Church of England, known as 'The Pilgrimage of Grace' valued at an annual rate of £1,700 sterling.

There the Lennoxes lived and where their first surviving son, Henry, who received the hereditary title of Lord Darnley, was born on 5 December 1545.

CHAPTER 2
Fear on the North Wind

The great central belt of Scotland runs from the east coast to the west, or vice versa in reverse. To the south lie the fertile Lowlands, to the north the mountains of the Highlands where life, precarious at its best, was threatened by both warfare and weather at its worst. March, officially the start of spring, was the nadir of all the hungry months following the harvests in autumn. The hills, brown with dead grass, and scorched by arctic winds running down to gentler ground in the glens below, showed nothing but a faint hint of green in sheltered south facing places on which deer and goats, their ribs showing plain beneath their now matted winter coats, could snatch a bit of grass. Starvation haunted the minds of both humans and animals as hail stones battered the ground. The beef tubs, filled with salted water as a preservative, were by that time nearly empty, the hay down to a few last musty piles. It was always a time of anxiety, but, in that early spring of 1544, there was a new great terror, insidious as the unseen blasts of wind scything down from the snow topped mountains to the north. War was coming between the Lord of Lennox and the Regent Earl of Arran.

The lairds of the Lennox, all of them vassals of the Earl, now returned to his own country kept men on constant sentry duty, watching from the towers of the castles for any sign of disturbance. Amongst them, south of Loch Lomond, were the Grahams of Montrose, the Douglasses of Mains, the Edmonstones of Duntreath and perhaps most importantly, as they were related to the powerful Earl of Glencairn, the Cunninghams of Drumquhassle.

This was a family whose fortalice of Drumquhassle (ridge of the castle) stood in the valley of the Endrick, a river famed for its late summer run of salmon, which rises at the back of the

Gargunnock Hills. Formed by the confluence of the Gourlay and Burnfoot burns, which join at a point about four-and-a-half miles south of the village of Kippen, to become the Endrick. From there the river runs in a westerly direction, bounding or traversing the parishes of Gargunnock, Fintry, Balfron, Killearn and Drymen, Buchananan and Kilmaronock, constituting Strathendrick. The name Endrick, deriving from the Gaelic 'avon ruadh', red river, from its colour when in flood, finally joins the south end of the great Highland waterway of Loch Lomond.

The Cunninghams of Drumquhassle, were descended, firstly from one of the younger sons of Sir Robert Cunningham of Kilmaurs and then later from the Cunninghams of Polmaise on the River Forth just to the east of the city of Stirling. In 1502, Alexander Cunningham, a younger son of Polmaise, through his marriage to Margaret Park had acquired three-quarters of the lands of Mugdock, lying just to the north of Milngavie, the rest of which belonged to the Graham Earl of Montrose. From Milngavie the Cunningham's land ran north-westward through what is now west Stirlingshire, above the Blane Valley encompassing the present day Stockiemuir Road, to the village of Drymen near where stood Drumquhassle Castle, on the northern edge of their territory.

Foremost among those summoned to arms was the Laird of Drumquhassle, A Cunningham, he was bound by loyalty to his chief William Cunningham, the Earl of Glencairn, as well as by his fealty to Matthew Earl of Lennox, superior of the district where he lived. Both of these men, by continuing to show support for the marriage of the little Mary Queen of Scots to Prince Edward, son of the English king, were in Scotland thought to be traitors. Lennox had written to Mary of Guise on 7 March, hoping to buy time by offering his innocence, suggesting a trial by a convention of his peers. He told her that he was suspected by the regent and his council 'that I am the principle man that causis division and brain be in this realm and makes daily insurrectionis and disobeance contrar the authority'.

Alexander and Margaret Cunningham's son Andrew had further advanced himself by his marriage to Mary, daughter of the 4th Lord Erskine. It was he, or their son John, who summoned by their overlord, Matthew Earl of Lennox, fought for Lennox and their Cunningham chief, the Earl of Glencairn in the fateful battle of Glasgow in March 1544.

Drumquhassle Castle, of which nothing now remains, about 1.5 miles to the east of the Stirlingshire village of Drymen, was once one among a line of fortresses sited strategically within sight of the line of Highland mountains from which robbers descended so regularly to steal and slaughter the cattle of the Lowland farms. A square built tower-house, three to four storeys in height, it would have been topped by the inevitable parapet wall from which sentries could keep constant watch. The ground floor would have contained vaulted cellars, large enough to hold the sacks of grain and casks of ale essential for the inmates of the castle to survive in the emergency of a siege. Above on the first floor was the dining hall, dominated by its great fireplace at one end, around which the entire household gathered to dine, and before which, when the trestle tables were cleared, many of the servants slept, their plaids wrapped round them, on the floor. The next floor housed the family bedrooms, where many of the beds were shared, and higher still were the attics beneath the slated roof.

Probably there was a courtyard into which cattle and sheep were driven for protection at first sight of raiders appearing from beyond the Highland range. Also within its precincts there would most likely have been a well, something essential for survival in the event of a prolonged attack. Extensions, on a lower scale to the tower, may have been added but, like most similar buildings, Drumquhassle Castle was constructed for defence rather than the comfort of its occupants.

Watching from the ramparts on an early March morning of 1544 was a young man, son of the laird, sent there by his father so that the man who normally stood watch could get on with the ploughing in a spell of dry weather. John Cunningham, leaning against the balustrade, was picking out moss from the stonework with the point of his dagger to subdue his feelings of rebellion against his parental orders which, although such a cause of boredom, he dared not disobey. With tears pricking at the back of his eyes at the sense of injustice inflicted upon him by being forced to stand idle and useless in a freezing wind when he could have been out flying his hawks, his mind was suddenly distracted by the thud of galloping hooves.

Glancing down from the battlements he saw a horseman riding hard towards the castle along the bank of the River Endrick stretching towards Loch Lomond in the west. The man carried saddle-bags and his horse was lathered. Plainly he brought important news. John scampered down the turnpike stair, yelling loudly for his father as he went.

Reaching the courtyard he dashed to hold the blowing horse as the man, throwing his leg across the bow of the saddle, dismounted in one leap. Unstrapping his saddle-bag he pulled out, not the papers that John expected to see but two joined pieces of charred wood. In a flash, John recognised the fiery cross, the age-long symbol of a summons to arms. The man gasped out that he came from Dumbarton Castle, sent by the Earl of Lennox to raise an army in his name. Then, in the same instance, his father, the laird, his boots encrusted with mud from his own work in the fields, entered the courtyard to take control.

John was told to saddle his pony and ride round to every farmhouse and labourer's cottage on the Drumquhassle estate to summon the men aged between sixteen and sixty to converge on the castle to be armed. Some of the men responded willingly, seeing a chance of gaining loot, always the perquisite of war. Others were less willing, dragged away from the patches of ground, just getting ready for planting, on which the living of them and their families depended for the coming year. In some places the women folk wailed pitifully, sacking aprons over their heads, as they bewailed the loss of their men. But nonetheless they came, the sturdy small men of the Lowlands, ploughmen rather than cattlemen, smaller of stature than most of the Highlanders, those scraggy, long-legged ruffians hardened by roaming the hills.

The laird let his farms to tenants, or tacksmen as they were called. Frequently relations, they paid their rent largely in kind and sub-let to smaller tenants or cotters in return for both labour and payment in produce, currency of the time. The tenants were also obliged by the rules of the age-old feudal system when summoned to rise in arms. Unwillingly, dragged away from the small patches of land and the few beasts on which their living depended, the fencible men – those between sixteen and sixty who were sound in mind and limb – had to come to wherever they were told to assemble, usually the forecourt or courtyard of the castle. The order to do so would, in the strath of the Endrick, come directly from the Earl of Lennox, superior of the district of his name, or, should he happen to be absent, from whoever was the factor or controller of the Lennox estates as Drumquhassle is later known to have been.

Meanwhile, on that March day of 1544 all was noise and bustle in the castle. Footsteps, clattering on the stone turnpike stair, echoed throughout the whole of the height and length of the building. Loudest of all was the voice of the lady of Drumquhassle, shouting at her husband to take plenty of provisions and warm clothes for the bairn. John himself, embarrassed by being called a child in front of his father's men, was busy being fitted with a steel breastplate, the smallest that could be found to fit him, amongst the ancient pieces of such protective equipment that had lain rusting in the armoury since the great emergency of the Field of Flodden when John's grandfather had led his men to fight for the present Queen's grandfather in the battle from which so few had returned. John's grandfather had been fortunate. One of the few to survive the appalling scrimmage in which King James himself had died.

Now with his breastplate and a small sword, also hastily scraped clean of rust, strapped to his side, John on his pony rode out of the courtyard, his head held high in pride.

Before him the few men who were mounted followed the unmistakeable figure of his father, riding the great grey mare taken from out of the plough team to be hastily rubbed down and saddled only the day before. Behind the horsemen came the men on foot, all of them wearing the hodden grey of the Lowlands and clasping an assortment of weapons, mainly pikes, bill-hooks and axes and in some cases even scythes.

In a party they marched to the city over the well-trodden track leading from the valley of the River Endrick up into the surrounding hills, the higher ground still brown with grass killed by wind and frost. After some fifteen miles smoke rising into the sky marked out the nearness of the city, the port of Glasgow built round the last navigable stretch of the River Clyde. Lennox's men were sent to occupy the Cathedral as the Hamilton Earl of Arran ordered cannons and muskets to be dragged across the central belt of Scotland from Edinburgh Castle to lay siege to Glasgow.

But it was not in the town that they fought but on the wild moorland a mile east of the city. A wide stretch of ground to the south of Campsie Fells, at this time in early spring alive with curlews, returning from winter hibernation on the coast, circling into the wind-blown sky, above reeds, bogs and thick heather, searching for nesting sites on the ground.

Screaming defiance the Lennox men charged forward to drive the first rank of their enemies back into the second and to capture their cannons. Triumphant, they waved their weapons to the sky but, almost in the same instant came the drum of massed hoof-beats as they felt the peaty ground shake beneath their feet. Two Lowland lairds, Robert Boyd of Kilmarnock and Mungo Mure of Rowallan, leading a small party of horsemen, charged into the ranks of the Lennox men and sent them running, clutching those same weapons that had just proclaimed their triumph held aloft.

The day was won for the Regent Hamilton Earl of Arran at the cost of some 300 lives on both sides. However, as Lennox then withdrew to his own great fortress of Dumbarton, Arran laid siege to Glasgow Castle, known as the Bishop's Palace. Siting his guns to blast against the walls of the palace, he took the town of Glasgow on 26 March.

On Lennox's garrison surrendering, gallows were set up in the street outside the Tolbooth on which the leaders, despite a promise of pardon, were hanged. According to the historian Pitscottie, the siege began on 28 March and lasted ten days, the captains of Glasgow Castle were won over with promises of gold and then, upon their surrender, hanged.[3]

Two months later, in May 1544, an English army sacked Edinburgh before, on about the 24th, Arran fought a second battle on Glasgow Moor, against William Cunningham, Earl of Glencairn, at the head of 500 vassals forced into service as his spearmen. In the conflict Glencairn's second son Andrew and Arran's Master of the Household, John Hamilton of Cambuskenneth were killed.

Most of the bodies, many without limbs or decapitated, were left lying on the open moor until at night the less respectable of Glasgow citizens crept out of the city, furtive as ghosts, to despoil them of anything they could find.

Whether or not John Cunningham of Drumquhassle and his father were involved in this second battle is unknown but it seems likely that, in view of the fact that they were Glencairn's kinsmen, this was probably the case. Certainly it is recorded that ten years later, those who received pardons for opposing the regent, included their Cunningham Chief Glencairn. Notable for his bravery, in the first conflict however, was Lennox's vassal Cunningham of Drumquhassle, something which Lennox himself would not forget.

CHAPTER 3
King Henry's Man

King Henry, who never did anything for nothing, was quick to make use of Matthew Lennox in his war against the Scots. Hardly had Matthew been married in August 1544 that Henry, by then himself fighting in France, made Matthew Lennox his lieutenant for the north of England and southern Scotland, where an English army, commanded by the Earl of Hereford, had already wrecked great devastation during the summer months.

Matthew sailed in a warship, which was part of a naval expedition, sent to support Hereford, by harrying Scotland's west coast. Landing at Dumbarton Castle he expected a welcome, but instead nearly lost his life. He was entering the hall when the captain of the castle suddenly drew his sword and demanded his surrender to the Scottish Government. Thanks to his secretary, Thomas Bishop, who, standing beside him, had the presence of mind to seize two pikes from the wall, both he and Matthew managed to beat off the attackers and to reach the safety of their ship lying at anchor out of gunshot of the cannon placed on the castle battlements.

Despatched to France to report what had happened to King Henry, who had just taken Boulogne, the secretary Bishop met with a sharp reproof.

Matthew Lennox then remained out of favour with the King, but on Henry's death, on 28 January 1547, the Lennoxes hastened to pay court to the son who succeeded him as Edward VI.

The Scottish ambassador in London sent urgent messages to the Regent Arran in Scotland telling him of renewed preparations for war. Early in September 1547 an army, composed partly of

German mercenaries, was led by Edward Seymour, Earl of Hereford, now made Duke of Somerset, into Scotland. On 10 September, Arran was totally defeated on the banks of the River Esk in what became known as the battle of Pinkie Heugh.

The struggle between the French and the English then accelerated as Arran tried desperately to get aid from the French king now, Henry II. But, in the vacuum of power, which followed the battle of Pinkie, the government in Scotland virtually lost control. The English, at the gates of Edinburgh, were threatening to bombard the city. Meanwhile, in Stirling Castle, the Dowager Queen, Mary of Guise, terrified that her five-year-old daughter, the little Queen Mary, would be kidnapped and taken to England, sent her for safety to the Benedictine Priory of Inchmahome, on an island in the Lake of Menteith. There she stayed for some weeks until, as the immediate crisis abated, it was thought safe enough for her to return to her mother in Stirling Castle.

Then at last, in the following June of 1548, in answer to Arran's near frantic supplications, a French force landed at Leith. The Scottish army, with French reinforcements, attempted to take the town of Haddington from the English and it was near here in a nunnery that, on 7 July 1548, an agreement was signed promising Mary as a bride to the dauphin, Henry II's son.

The French fleet then again put out to sea, to sail round the north coast of Scotland and down the west to Dumbarton, where, at the end of July, the little queen, together with her 'Four Marys', embarked to sail safely for France. Seven months later, in February 1549, in reward for his part in arranging the marriage of his sovereign to the heir of France, Arran was rewarded with the Dukedom of Châtelhérault by King Henry II.

In the same month Matthew Lennox, now in charge of part of the English army, marched west to destroy the town of Annan in Dumfriesshire, before being defeated in an attempt to take Dumfries. Infuriated by his failure and goaded on by his secretary, Bishop, Matthew ordered the hanging of several young boys, sons of the local landowners who had defied him, an atrocity which was to haunt him for the rest of his life.

Never distinguished in army command, he returned to his Yorkshire estate to live there, when not attending the courts of King Henry's three successors, until sent back to Scotland by Queen Elizabeth. The conflict between England and Scotland, known as the 'War of the Rough Wooing' which ended in March 1551 was finalised by the treaty, signed between England and Scotland, in June 1551.

Relations between the two countries then improved to the extent, that in October 1551, a mere four months after the agreement of the truce, the Regent Arran, now a French duke, requested a passport through England for a young man, known as the Laird of Drumquhassle, together with six companions, to travel through England on his way to France. Why one wonders did they go? Was it in the hope of finding employment as mercenary soldiers, like so many young men from Scotland at the time? Or were they sent to conduct some form of business on the regent's newly acquired French estate? Alternately, did they travel at the behest of the Earl of Mar, uncle of Drumquhassle, a relation later known to have greatly advanced his career? This, the second mention of a Scottish laird of relatively small importance, is nonetheless significant of the sinister happenings in Scottish history in which he was to play a major part.

It was certainly John, who, sometime prior to 1548, succeeded his father as the third laird of Drumquhassle. On his return from France (on the passport organised by the regent) he successfully married a cousin, co-heiress of her father's estate of Polmaise. Possibly using her lands as collateral, they then contrived to buy out her sisters' (Margaret and Katherine) in a deed dated 27 May 1556. Such was the value of their property that Drumquhassle was then made a barony, with the right to hold baron's courts, Drumquhassle Castle, being its main seat.[4]

That Drumquhassle had now become a man of some influence is shown by his presence in the Reformation Parliament of August 1560. This proved to be the Revolutionary Assembly, which on 17 August, accepted the hotly-debated reformed Confession of Faith. Papal authority was denounced on

24 August, and the celebration of Mass became a criminal offence.

In the following year, Drumquhassle is noted as a member of his cousin Lord Mar's garrison of Edinburgh Castle when he was involved in a debate on the artillery. More significantly, he would be present at the General Assembly of the Church of Scotland of June 1567, when Scotland's future as a Protestant country, governed by a Protestant King would be enacted.

But that King, as yet, remained unborn.

CHAPTER 4
Return to Scotland

Mary Queen of Scots, a widow at nineteen after her brief marriage to King Francis II of France had ended with his death, came back to Scotland, landing at Leith, on 19 August 1561. Amongst those watching as she came ashore were some, who remembering her mother, Mary of Guise, rejoiced at the similarity of their features and at what was then so unusual for a woman, their outstanding height. Queen Mary, in token of her widowhood, wore black and there were some who muttered at the sight of it, foretelling as they believed bad luck, as did the thick mist, driven in by the wind from the North Sea, which to the superstitious folk, attending their new sovereign's arrival, was a certain portent of disaster. Nonetheless it was a joyous cavalcade that rode from the port of Leith towards the just visible focal point of Arthur's Seat, rising above the Palace of Holyroodhouse.

It was three years later, in September 1564, that Matthew, Earl of Lennox, also returned from England to Scotland, permitted by Queen Elizabeth to attempt to reclaim his Scottish estates, forfeited by the Scottish government for his adherence to her father, Henry VIII. It was largely thanks to the diplomacy of the Melvilles, the diplomats Sir James and his brother Robert, that Lennox was restored to his lands and titles by proclamation of a herald at the Mercat Cross in Edinburgh, on 9 October 1564.

It seems probable, if not provable, that it was at this point that, perhaps on the advice of Lord Erskine, unused as he was to Scottish procedures, that Lennox employed that nobleman's cousin as general factotum of his estates.

John Cunningham, the laird of Drumquhassle, as he was most commonly known, had certainly proved himself competent both in the organisation, and the acquisition and distribution of arms to the garrison of Edinburgh Castle over which his cousin, Lord Erskine, had command. But even had he not been recommended to him, Lennox must have remembered the father (or it may even have been John himself, such is the vagueness regarding their ages) who had fought so gallantly for him at the Battle of Glasgow in the March of 1544. Then it had been, that after sailing from Dumbarton, he had escaped from Scotland to find sanctuary in England under King Henry's rule.

All that is known for certain, is that it was about this time, or shortly afterwards, that John Cunningham of Drumquhassle became "Baillie, Chamberlain, Receiver of the Earldom of Lennox and Lordship of Darnley, effectively the Earl of Lennox's right-hand man, responsible for the Earl's financial matters."[5]

Not everyone was pleased with this arrangement. Sir James Melville describes Drumquhassle as 'ambitious, and greedy, his greatest care was to advance himself and his friends.' [6] Nonetheless, despite his faults he was efficient to the point where his appointment as factor, or estate manager, proved only to be first step in what seemed to be an unstoppable rise to power.

Lennox had only been in Scotland for little more than a year before he was joined by his son Henry, Lord Darnley, a young man of twenty, who was noticeable for his height. Queen Elizabeth, who called him 'yon long lad' was furious, having not given him licence to leave England. Taking revenge against his mother, the Lady Lennox who had begun life as Margaret Douglas, daughter of Queen Margaret Tudor by her second marriage to the Earl of Angus, she put her in the Tower of London. But there was nothing she could do to prevent Henry Darnley's marriage to Queen Mary, which took place in the private chapel at Holyrood on 29 July 1565.

By the autumn, it was known that the Queen was pregnant. The dynasty of Scotland's royal family seemed secured.

From Scotland Matthew Lennox wrote continuously to his wife Margaret, giving her news of all that was taking place. Unusually for those times amongst the aristocracy they addressed each other by their Christian names, he even used a nick-name betokening the great affection he is known to have had for Margaret, harridan of her household as she may have been. Dating a letter from his house in Glasgow, on 19 December 1565, he told her what she most wanted to hear.

Addressing her as 'My sweet Madge' he first apologised for his delay in writing to her, due as he explained, to the time-absorbing pressure of all that was taking place. Then, knowing how it would please her, he broke the wonderful news:

"My Madge, we have to give God most hearty thanks for that the King, our son, continues in good health, and the Queen is great with child (God save them all) for which cause we have great cause to rejoice the more."[7]

HOLYROOD PALACE – SATURDAY 9 MARCH 1567

Had the pistol fired he would have died three months before he was due to be born. It was only thanks to the inexcusable latitude of Kerr of Fawdonside in maintaining his rather ancient weapon that the explosion, which he waited for... became nothing but a gentle click.

King James's first, pre-natal brush with death took place in his mother's apartments on the second floor of the north-west corner of Holyrood Palace. The lay-out consisted of four rooms, a large presence chamber, an equally big bedroom just off it and next to that, again, two very small rooms, one a dressing room, the other a supper room. Down one storey, immediately below and of much the same dimensions, were the rooms currently occupied by Henry Lord Darnley, father of the yet unborn child of Mary Queen of Scots.

The two almost identical sets of apartments were connected by a staircase, ending in the Queen's bedroom close to the supper room wherein, on the evening of Saturday 9 March 1567, Queen Mary sat with a close circle of friends. Her guests on that evening were her illegitimate brother and sister, Lord Robert Stuart and Lady Jean Stewart, the Countess of Argyll, and two members of her household, Robert Beaton, the Laird of Creich and Sir Arthur Erskine, her Master of Horse. The Queen sat at the head of the table while at the foot was David Rizzio, her Italian secretary, splendidly dressed in a gown of damask trimmed with fur, a satin doublet and hose of russet velvet. Arrogant, he wore a cap on his head, flaunting his favouritism, in defiance of the protocol

33

demanding that heads should always be uncovered in the presence of the Queen.

The supper was in progress when, up the private stair, came Darnley to put his arm around her and sit himself beside the Queen. This was a surprise to all those gathered round the table for it was known, that the two, if not exactly at loggerheads, had of recent been quarrelling over the vexed question of the Mary refusing to grant her husband the one thing he desired above all others; his promised matrimonial Crown.

Nonetheless his wife seemed pleased enough to see him, asking if he had supped, to which he replied that he had already done so and wanted only her company rather than anything to eat. He did, however seem nervous, constantly glancing over his shoulder until from below, came the heavy tread of steel-clad footsteps ascending the adjacent stair.

Suddenly, there were gasps of horror as a bizarre figure, wearing of all things, a nightgown over full armour, staggered into the room. He might well have been a ghost but was recognised as Lord Ruthven who, suffering from what on his own account was inflammation of the liver and consumption of the kidneys, had for weeks been extremely ill.

In the silence which followed his entrance, Ruthven pointed at Rizzio and in a voice hardly above a whisper said, "Let it please your Majesty that yonder man David come forth of your privy chamber where he has been over long."

Queen Mary, quick to gather her wits, turned to face this spectre demanding, "What offence hath he done?"

Ruthven replied, "He hath offended your honour, which I dare not be so bold as to speak of. As to your husband's honour, he hath hindered him of the Crown Matrimonial, which your Grace promised him, besides many other things…"

Hardly had these words been spoken before chaos erupted in the room. Rizzio ran round the table to crouch behind the Queen clutching at her skirts. Creich and Erskine drew their daggers as Ruthven said to Darnley, "Sir! Take the Queen your wife and sovereign to you," while shouting at Creich and Erskine, "Lay no hands on me for I will not be handled."

Then more armed men rushed up the stairs to burst into the already crowded room. The table over-turned and went flying: the Countess of Argyll the only one present with enough presence of mind to seize one of the candlesticks. Ruthven pushed the Queen into the arms of Darnley, who held her, struggling like a maniac, in a stranglehold embrace. She felt the tug as Rizzio's fingers were prized from her skirt as he was pulled away, screaming: "Madame! Save ma vie! Save ma vie!" But she could do nothing to help him, pinioned as she was against the breastplate on Darnley's chest. Breathless, squirming in fury, she could only listen as, with fifty-six strokes of daggers, her little Italian secretary, dragged from the room, was brutally stabbed to death.

It was at this moment that Patrick Bellenden and Andrew Ker of Fawdonside held their pistols to Queen Mary's swollen stomach. Ker's finger, resting on the trigger, pulled it back, holding his breath for the explosion, until, above the clamour, he heard only a slight scraping sound as the weapon misfired. Bellenden, losing his nerve, then pulled his pistol away. King James VI of Scotland, alive but as yet unborn, had survived the first of many attempts made against his life.

CHAPTER 5
A Prince Is Born

In a tiny panelled room in Edinburgh Castle, at about ten o'clock on the morning of 19 June 1566, King James VI of Scotland and later 1st of England, came howling into the world. The Queen had endured a long and painful labour, during which the right foot of the infant somehow became trapped so that thereafter it always turned out, giving him an odd and apparently unbalanced walk. Despite this the baby seemed healthy and in fact a beautiful child, as was reported to an envious Queen Elizabeth by her ambassador, Sir Henry Killigrew.

James remained in Edinburgh, cared for by Lady Reres and his wet-nurse, a woman called Helena Little, who, like many of her kind, was said to be a drunkard, together with many other attendants until in late August, when he was two months old, his mother had him transferred to Stirling Castle, traditional nursery of Scottish princes. His cortège set off attended by five hundred harquebusiers, who escorted him to Stirling where he was given into the care of the Earl of Mar, hereditary governor of the castle.[8]

No money was spared in preparing the prince's nursery, arranged entirely by his mother. Buckets of gold and silver were ordered, together with lengths of blue plaiding for his cradle, fustian for his mattress, blankets and feathers for his bolster. Tapestry lined the walls, precluding draughts through cracks in the stone.[9]

Her son's nursery arranged, Queen Mary turned her mind to his christening, an event of prestigious importance in Scotland as elsewhere in the Catholic countries of Western Europe as well as in Protestant England. From here the baby's cousin, the childless Queen Elizabeth, as his godmother sent a gift of a splendid gold font, weighing 333 ounces and decorated with jewels and enamel "so designed that the whole effect combine elegance with value."[10] Other gifts included a necklace and earrings of pearls and rubies, brought by the French ambassador the Compte de Brienne from Charles IX, the King of France and a big fan of jewelled feathers, worth four thousand crowns carried to Scotland (too late for the event) by the ambassador of Emmanuel Philibert, the Duke of Savoy.

The christening took place in the Royal Chapel of Stirling Castle on Tuesday 17 December 1566, the fact of it not happening until Prince James was six months old, providing the best indication of his being a healthy child. Normally infant mortality was then so common that babies were hastily baptised on the day following their birth, it then being thought that human beings were without a soul until the ceremony was performed.

It was nearly dark on that late winter's day when the baby, dressed in a family christening robe, quite an armful at the age of six months, was carried from his nursery in the royal apartments across the courtyard to the Chapel Royal of Stirling Castle by the Count de Brienne, standing proxy for the prince's godfather, Charles IX King of France. Walking carefully over the cobbles, already slippery with frost, he was flanked by two rows of barons and gentlemen each holding a lighted wax candle in his hand. Behind followed the Earl of Atholl, bearing a large wax candle, the Earl of Eglinton, carrying the salt, Lord Sempill, the rood (cross) and Lord Ross, the ewer and basin.

At the door of the chapel waited Archbishop Hamilton, the illegitimate brother of James Earl of Arran, Duc de Châtelhérault. Hamilton, with the assistance of other bishops, was to baptise the little prince, but the Queen, knowing that he had recently received treatment for venereal disease, had specifically forbidden him to spit in the baby's mouth, as then was customary in Catholic ritual. James was to claim afterwards, apparently with some pride, that his mother had insisted that she would not have "a pocky priest spitting in her child's mouth."

At the font he was held by his aunt, the Countess of Argyll, standing proxy for his godmother Queen Elizabeth. The Archbishop christened him Charles James, after the King of France and the line of his ancestors, the Stewart Kings of Scotland. Following the ceremony the trumpets blew a joyous fanfare of salute. The prince's names and titles were proclaimed three times by heralds; "Charles James, James Charles, Prince and Steward of Scotland, Duke of Rothesay, Earl of Carrick, Lord of the Isles and Baron of Renfrew." Then did the music begin and continued for some time until the prince was carried back to his nursery.

Most noticeable of all by his absence was the child's father Henry Darnley. A splendid suit had been designed for him, glittering in cloth of gold. But he was sulking, grossly offended, because to add to what he felt were the many indignities thrust upon him, Queen Elizabeth was now refusing to acknowledge him as King of Scotland so that her ambassador, the Earl of Bedford, would address him merely as Lord Darnley, an insult he could not face.

Following the christening the festivities included a banquet with a Latin masque by George Buchanan, the Scottish historian and humanist scholar, who was to prove such a determining factor in the future education of the baby for whom the celebrations were held. Born in the old house called the Moss, in the west Stirlingshire Parish of Killearn, Buchanan was a man of the Lennox, owing fealty to Darnley's father, the Earl of Lennox and for this reason protective of Darnley against what he thought to be the calumnies of his wife, Queen Mary. Matters between the royal couple, their relationship by this time clearly strained, culminated in crisis when, on 24 December, Mary pardoned the murderers of Rizzio with the exception only of Ker of Fawdonside and George Douglas, the Postulate of Arbroath, whom she believed had threatened her own life. These were the men betrayed by Darnley, who in consequence feared for his life.

His father, Matthew, Lord Lennox, claimed afterwards that he himself had sent the warning to his son that the Queen and her councillors, at a conference held at Craigmillar Castle, had agreed that Darnley should be arrested and imprisoned. [11] Believing himself in danger, he called for his horse to be saddled and without a word to his wife, left Stirling the same night aiming for his father's house in Glasgow where he believed he would be safe. But only a mile beyond Stirling, he doubled up in the saddle, convulsed with appalling pain. Somehow his servants conveyed him to Glasgow, probably in a horse-drawn litter, a distance of some twenty-five miles. Arriving there the blisters broke out, reportedly of a bluish colour, which the doctors at once said proved poison. Subsequently, however, their diagnosis changed, as they attributed the pustules to small-pox, a disease most virulent at the time. It is now commonly thought that he was suffering from syphilis, contracted while, as a young man, he had spent some time in France.

Meanwhile in Stirling, Queen Mary became increasingly concerned over the safety of her son. The castle, massive fortress as it was, was dangerously close to the great region of the Lennox, stronghold of Darnley's family where the land holders were vassals to a man.

Already, Mary had heard rumours sent by Archbishop Beaton, her ambassador to Paris, that there was a plot against her forming in Scotland organised by her husband's supporters. Darnley was supposed to have a boat ready and waiting to take him out of the country. It was not beyond the bounds of possibility that he would try to abduct his little son from Stirling Castle and take him to France.

Thoroughly alarmed, on 14 January 1567 (Gregorian Calendar) Queen Mary had her baby son removed from Stirling and taken back to Holyrood, where she is said to have slept with him in his cradle (perhaps the one still kept at Traquair House) in her bedroom. Anxiously she watched over him. It was a short time which she would remember for ever, but of which he had no recollection in his still irretentive mind.

On 20 January Queen Mary set off for Glasgow to bring her husband, now slowly recovering from his illness, back to Edinburgh in a horse-drawn litter. It was partly for fear of infection, affecting the little Prince James, that he was lodged in the old Provost's lodging of Kirk o'Field, a house of medium size, built just inside the city wall, standing within a quadrangle attached to the old collegiate church of St Mary-in-the-Fields.

It is fortunate that James, who was later renowned for his horror of bloodshed, was so young as to be oblivious to the dreadful events of the next few days, which in the early hours of Monday 10 February, ended in his father's death by strangulation.

It was over a month later, sometime towards the end of March, that the little boy was returned to his royal nursery in Stirling Castle. Escorted by the Earls of Argyll and Huntly, the now nine-month-old child was received by the Earl of Mar, Governor of the Castle.

On Monday 21 April Queen Mary, who had had ridden by stages from Seton Palace, reached Stirling Castle to see her son. The visit was made in secret, she being attended only by her secretary, Sir William Maitland of Lethington, the Earl of Huntly and the contemporary historian Sir James Melville.[12] For all of the next day of Tuesday she played with little James, while she marvelled at how he had grown. But on Wednesday she had to leave, to begin the ride back to Edinburgh and attend to matters of state. She was not to know when she left him, perhaps lifting him from his crib to hold his warm little body close to her own, that she would never see him again.

CHAPTER 6
The Guardian

It is fortunate for posterity that Sir James Melville, the diplomat and recorder of his times, was amongst the armed escort that escorted Queen Mary back to Edinburgh. It is he who has left such a revealing picture of a young woman—she was still only twenty-four—reduced by physical illness and mental misery to a shadow of the vibrant being who, only six years earlier, had come to Scotland from France. On leaving Stirling she had not gone far before she felt so violently ill that she had to dismount and be taken into a nearby cottage to rest.

Recovered to some extent she then remounted and was some way between Edinburgh and Linlithgow when, as Sir James describes, "the Earl of Bothwell recounted her with a great company and took her Majesty's horse by the bridle; his men took the Earl of Huntly, the secretary Lethington and me, and carried us captives to Dunbar; all the rest were permitted to go free. Then the Earl of Bothwell boasted he would marry the queen, who would or who would not; yea whether she would herself or not. Captain Blackater, who had taken me, alleged that it was with the Queen's own consent. The next day in Dunbar I obtained permission to go home."[13]

Melville was lucky indeed. Bothwell was merciless in disposing of anyone whom he took to be a threat. Lethington alone survived being done to death by the Earl's dagger in the Queen's own chamber, by Mary standing between them and telling William Maitland of Lethington to be gone which he did with all possible speed. Melville likewise made himself scarce, but he was there, in the Great Hall of Holyrood Palace when, in a Protestant ceremony, Mary married Bothwell on 15 May 1567.

Hardly was the service over, however before Bothwell, by this time created Duke of Orkney, began trying to achieve

41

supreme power by getting the Prince into his hands. Furious, he found himself thwarted by the Earl of Mar, who, as Melville wrote:

"Was a true nobleman [and] would not deliver him out of his custody, alleging that he could not without the consent of the three estates; yet he was so oft pressed by them that had the authority in their hands, that he was put to great strait, after that he had made divers refusals; among others he made his moan to me, praying me to help to save the prince out of their hands who had slain his father and had already made his vaunt among his familiars that if he could get him once into his hands, he would warrant him from revenging his father's death. I said that I would wish it lay in my power to make my help in that; he asked me if I could find any out gate [solution]. I answered that I was intimately acquainted with Sir James Balfour, and that I knew how matters stood between Bothwell and him."[14]

Sir James goes on to explain that he had heard, through the laird of Whitelaw, that there were, "some jealousies and suspicions arisen betwixt them" and that Bothwell was determined to have the control of Edinburgh Castle, of which Sir James Balfour was the governor, out of his hands. Balfour had formally been a close friend of Bothwell, as indeed of the Queen, but he openly defied him by refusing to have anything to do with "the murderers of the king." Bothwell, enraged, was then determined to have him out of Edinburgh Castle in which he was going to put his henchmen, a Hepburn who was laird of Beinston, in his place.

This gave Mar a chance to prevaricate "that he saw not a sure house to keep the prince in case he would deliver him." Whereupon, Melville himself returned to Edinburgh specifically to tell Sir James Balfour on no account to part with the castle, "whereby he might be an instrument to save not only the Prince but the Queen, who was now in a pitiful state."

Melville does not say how he got access to Holyrood, presumably he seized the opportunity having been told, perhaps by one of the guards, that Bothwell had ridden out. Somehow he managed to see the Queen and heard her in front of her equerry Arthur Erskine, ask for a knife to stab herself, "or else I shall drown myself."[15] Greatly distressed, Melville told Sir James Balfour, that however he was putting himself at risk, he must continue to hold Edinburgh Castle, not only to save the Queen and the Prince and to assist the nobles who were about to crown him, but "to pursue the Earl of Bothwell for the King's murder."

Melville then assured him that this was the only way that he would escape the taint of involvement in Darnley's death, on the known suspicion of his former friendship with Bothwell, assuring him that he had it from Whitelaw, the Captain of the castle of Dunbar, that Bothwell was determined to take Edinburgh Castle from him, install the laird of Beinston in his place, and put the Prince there in his keeping. Sir James Balfour then agreed to do this on condition that he had the protection of the man soon to prove himself the Queen's champion, Sir William Kirkaldy of Grange.

Meanwhile, Alexander Erskine, brother of the Earl of Mar, came in secret to Melville in the dead of night. He told him that his brother was continually being threatened by Bothwell, who demanded that he should release Prince James to him. Mar was continuing to dissemble, saying that he would only do what Bothwell demanded: "Once an honest and responsible nobleman had been made governor of Edinburgh Castle, and the nobility might have gathered to pursue the murderers and crown the Prince, as at a secret meeting had already been arranged." [16]

It was word of a plot against him, perhaps deliberately leaked, that Holyrood was to be surrounded with the aim of taking him prisoner, that made Bothwell lose his nerve. Taking the Queen with him, he fled from Edinburgh, first to the castle of Borthwick, and from there to the even stronger sea girt fortress of Dunbar, granted to him by Mary, whom he held there as his captive until she escaped disguised as a man.

Her subsequent story; her defeat by the army of Protestant lords, and desertion by Bothwell at the nearby Carberry Hill, her imprisonment on Loch Leven, her escape and flight into England, have already been told many times. To her little son, James, now just thirteen months old, safe in the environment of Stirling Castle, guarded by the man whom his mother had appointed to protect him and who had so cleverly and resolutely outwitted the attempts to abduct him, it all meant nothing at all.

Margaret, Countess of Lennox, was still in the Tower of London when told of her son's death. Hysterical with grief, she was so ill that Queen Elizabeth, assured that she was dying, relented her harsh treatment to send her own physician, Doctor Huick and the Dean of Westminster to minister to her in the Tower. Subsequently, on the advice of the Queen's secretary William Cecil, who pointed out that as Margaret believed that Queen Mary had been at least partly responsible for the murder of her son, she would in no way try to communicate with her, Elizabeth allowed that the bereaved mother should be released from the Tower.

Back at Temple Newsan, the house granted to them by Queen Elizabeth in Yorkshire near Leeds, she was joined by Matthew, returned from Scotland, a man so bent and aged by grief that he was barely recognisable even to the wife and children he had left behind when he had ridden to the court of the young Queen a mere four years ago. Obsessed with loathing for Henry Darnley's murderers, Matthew, before leaving Edinburgh had organised a hate campaign. Placards, depicting Bothwell, were nailed up throughout the city some labelled, "Here is the murderer of the King," while others read, "Farewell gentle Henry, but a vengeance on Mary." At night, as darkness fell, a ghostly figure walked the streets crying out that Bothwell had murdered the King, while unearthly voices wailed for vengeance on his death.

Lennox had left Scotland before, in December of that fateful year of 1567, the Scottish Parliament issued a warrant for Bothwell's arrest on a charge of involvement in the murder of Henry Darnley, consort of the now imprisoned Queen. Absent in person, Lennox's influence was nonetheless paramount in that, foremost amongst those instrumental in ordering the Earl's arrest, was a man, hitherto of little significance, but now noticeably climbing up the ladder of influence as the factor and chief administrator of the great Lennox estates. John Cunningham, the laird of Drumquhassle, now suddenly of some consequence, was acting on the orders of Lennox, his liege lord, a man obsessed in seeing justice executed on Bothwell whom he believed to have been responsible for the killing of his adored eldest son.

Queen Mary was already a prisoner, forced to abdicate in favour of her son when, on 29 July 1567, James was brought to the Protestant Church of the Holyrood, just below Stirling Castle, for his coronation. The full protocol was followed as the assembled company and one bewildered little boy listened to a sermon preached by John Knox. Then followed the reading of the Queen's commissions, which included the inauguration of the King's uncle, James Earl of Moray (who as half-brother of his mother Queen Mary, was the illegitimate son of James's grandfather James V) as regent during his nephew's minority.

However, it was the Earl of Morton, a large man, his face half-covered by a red beard, who took the coronation oath, "to reule in ye faith, fear and love of God, and maintain ye religion then professed in Scotland" on behalf of the child King.

It was Robert Stuart, Bishop of Orkney, brother of his grandfather and thus great uncle of James who crowned the little boy, presumably holding the crown just above the tiny head, which would otherwise have disappeared inside it. He then anointed him, on the top of his head, shoulder blades and palms of his hands, saying prayers before him in the English, or Scottish tongue. The royal robe was put on him, or rather draped across his shoulders. Then, in another symbolic gesture, a sword, which he was not allowed to touch, was put at his side, his fingers prized open to cover at least part of the sceptre with his tiny fist. Finally, as the Bishop pronounced the blessing, the service came to an end.

James was then carried back up the steep hill to Stirling Castle, while as the cannons fired a salute, his subjects regaled themselves with feasting, and letting off fireworks, which, if held up to a window to see them and if not too terrified of the noise, he may have been allowed to watch. Bemused as he was over all that was taking place, the boy in his nursery high in the tower, unlike those celebrating in the town of Stirling below, was unaware that he himself was the cause of so much joy.

CHAPTER 7
Of Charlatans and Mentors

And what was life like for that small motherless boy within the grim confines of Stirling Castle? Caroline Bingham, in her delightful book 'The makings of a King,' has left a revealing picture of the bedroom in which he slept, so different to the child's room of today. Now, when there would be cuddly toys and pictures, attractive to children, on the walls, then there were only tapestries, which flapped in the downdraught of the chimney, when, as so often happened, gusts of choking soot filled the room. Admittedly the tapestries, when on calm days hanging straight, depicting medieval huntsmen and their dogs and horses with possibly a castle in the background, did at least add a bit of colour to the otherwise starkness of the room.

Once too big for his cradle, James slept in a tower room of the castle, a tiny figure in a vast four poster bed, with hangings of black damask and on the bed itself a black fringed pillow. It was all part of his upbringing designed to drive the extravagancies of the Roman Catholic religion from his mind. James was to be a Protestant, a stalwart leader of the rigorous faith, which allowed no idolatry, in the form of crucifixes, rosaries and incense to divert him from the purity and rigour of the Calvinistic dictum. He was taught to hate the mother, whom he could not even remember, and all that she stood for, her religion in particular being described as that inspired by the devil's tongue.

Yet despite the many disadvantages of his surroundings and in particular the lack of affection, for which he is known to have craved, James was at least fortunate in that the man appointed to be his guardian was the governor of the castle, the Earl of Mar.

John, 19th Earl of Mar was descended from the Mormaers, or Great Stewards of Scotland. Donald Mormaer of Mar had fallen at the battle of Clontarf in 1014. It was Alexander I of Scotland, who reigned from 1107-1124, who had replaced the old Celtic system with the feudal one of creating Earls or Comes. Thus the Mormaer of Mar, at the founding of the Abbey of Scone in 1114, had been described as *Rothri Comes.*

Thirteen more Earls had followed until, in 1457, the title and a large part of the lands were illegally seized by King James II on the pretext that following the death of the 13th holder they had devolved upon the Crown.

The 15th, 16th and 17th lawful Earls of Mar were then known simply as Lords Erskine until, a hundred and ten years since they were disowned, fortune favoured the family in the person of the 18th rightful holder of the title so wrongly withheld.

John Erskine was a son of the 5th Lord Erskine, also named John, who had been both the guardian of King James V and afterwards of the latter's daughter, Mary Queen of Scots. Succeeding his father as 6th Lord Erskine, in 1552, this second John was Commendator, or Lay Administrator, of the great border foundation of Dryburgh Abbey, from 1547. Although adhering to the reformed religion, he was never zealous in its cause, although his was amongst the signatures on the letter asking the then exiled John Knox to return to Scotland in 1557.

As Governor of Edinburgh Castle during the years, when following the death of her husband James V, Mary of Guise had ruled as regent, Mar had struggled with the Lords of the Congregation and been largely instrumental in obtaining an uncertain peace between religious opponents. Then, when Queen Mary herself had returned to Scotland in 1561, when still Lord Erskine, Mar as a member of her council, had encouraged her marriage to her cousin, the young Lord Darnley, he being one of the men in Scotland who favoured what, at the time of its happening, had seemed such a suitable match. It was four years later when, in honour of his services, Erskine had been re-created Earl of Mar.

A stout-hearted, sensible man, his features largely concealed by an enormous beard, John Mar was the antithesis of his wife, Annabella Murray, daughter of William Murray of Tullibardine, whose strong temper and lively wit contrasted strongly with the stable demeanour of her spouse. Perhaps it was the attraction of opposites which had first drawn them together, but from every account it seems that the marriage was harmonious albeit if, as seems likely, Annabella was the dominant force.

There is little, if any doubt, that while it was Mar who defeated the attempts of the Earl of Bothwell, following his marriage to the Queen, to get the little Prince James under his control, it was his wife, the quick-witted and resourceful Annabella, who would have proved more than a match for Bothwell had he even attempted such a coup.

She certainly had the measure of George Buchanan, the Scottish historian and humanist, follower of John Knox, who was appointed as tutor to the young prince. Buchanan, now in his sixties, emaciated and in one of his later portraits, wearing a cowl over his presumably bald head, must have been a terrifying sight to the child as he drilled into him the Latin texts which proved the basis of the classical education for which he was later so renowned. But Buchanan was also a sadist, subjecting the little boy to beatings, until one day, unwise enough to ignore the approaching rustle of skirts across the floor, his raised arm was seized and jerked above his head as he was caught in the act by Lady Mar.

What then ensued between them history does not reveal. Buchanan got his own back by labelling Annabella "a very Jezebel and a sweet titbit for the devil's mouth." But Prince James, although plainly in awe of her and always in public addressing her as 'my Lady Mar,' afterwards sometimes called her 'Minnie' in the correspondence between them that lasted throughout many years.

Also of influence in the prince's upbringing was Alexander Erskine, his guardian's brother. Described by Melville as:

"a nobleman of a true, gentle nature, well liked and loved by all men for his good qualities and great discretion, no ways factious or envious, a lover of all honest men, and desired to see men of good conversation about the Prince, rather than his own nearer friends if he thought them not so meet."[17]

It may have been thanks to him that a second tutor, a young man named Peter Young, was introduced to teach James. There is, however, evidence to suggest that it was actually Buchanan who activated the appointment of what he called, "an upright and learned young man who [had been] for a long time very dear to me," apparently an indication of respect for his intellect, rather than of homosexual desire. Peter Young, who was twenty-seven, had studied in Geneva under Theodore Beza, the French Protestant Christian theologian, who, as the friend and successor of Calvin, had played such a leading part in the Reformation.

Peter Young, a gentle man in contrast to Buchanan, soon won the affection of his lonely little pupil. Sir James Melville, describing the different methods of the teachers, wrote that:

"Mr George was a stoick philosopher, who looked not far before him: a man of notable endowments for his learning and knowledge of Latin poesy, much honoured in other countries, pleasant in conversation, rehearsing at all occasions moralities short and instructive, whereof he had abundance; inventing where he wanted. He was also religious, but was easily abused, and so facile that he was led by every company he haunted, which made him factious in his old days, for he spoke and wrote as those who were about him for the time informed him, he was become slippery and careless, following in many things the vulgar opinion; for he was naturally popular, and extremely revengeful against any man who had offended him, which was his greatest fault."[18]

Melville then gave a rather amusing example of Buchanan's propensity to take offence, writing that: 'Although formally the Earl of Morton's greatest friend, he became his greatest enemy after, a hackney 'so sure-footed and easy' that it was one of his favourite horses, stolen so he claimed from a plainly dishonest servant, had been bought by Morton who refused to return it, after which there was nothing too bad that he could say of him.'

Likewise did John Cunningham, the Stirlingshire laird of Drumquhassle, much in attendance on his cousin Lord Mar, nurse a great hatred for Morton 'because the regent kept all casualties (property and revenue accruing to the crown) to himself, and would let nothing fall to others who were about the King, also become his great enemy; and so did they all that were about His Majesty' as Melville described.[19]

In contrast to George Buchan, Mr Peter Young was gentler, and was loth to offend the King at any time, and used himself warily, as a man who had a mind of his own weal, by keeping up his Majesty's favour. James remained on good terms with him in coming years, rewarding him with many favours.

James was not yet two, when, in May 1568, his mother escaped from her prison in Lochleven Castle and defeated by her half-brother, the Regent Moray, at Langside, near Glasgow, fled in a fishing boat across the Solway Firth to throw herself at the mercy of her cousin, Queen Elizabeth of England.

Moray, as regent, had to struggle against the hatred of the Hamiltons, the head of the house, the Duke of Châtelhérault, refusing to accept his authority, believing himself as a previous regent, to be entitled to that position. Supporting the Duke were his two sons, Lord John and Lord Claud Hamilton, but most importantly his illegitimate brother, John Hamilton, Bishop of St Andrews, the man who had baptised James. The bishop, although a clever man who, according to Lord Herries, "spent the least pairt of his tyme in spiritual contemplations [and] willinglie took pairt with his friends and kindred in all there ingadgements; for which cause, joined with his place of professioun, was more hated by the King's party the most of all the rest."[20]

In January 1570, after Moray had failed to capture Dumbarton Castle, held by her supporters for the imprisoned Queen, he returned to Stirling where, on Thursday 19th, he had invited English visitors, Sir Henry Gate, Marshal of Berwick and Sir William Drury to dine in the Great Hall. Prince James, at three years old, would have been too young to attend the banquet, but no doubt his uncle climbed up the spiral stair to his nursery to see for himself how his nephew was growing and progressing with the tutors employed to begin his education. He cannot have been disappointed. James was a lively and intelligent child, if inhibited in his physical development by the rickets, which through lack of enough nutrients are said to have resulted in bandy legs.

James was not to know, and neither did it appear his uncle, that his mother had recently tried to send him a present which, thanks to Queen Elizabeth, had failed to arrive. Mary had in fact sent him a small pony, together with its own diminutive saddle, which came with a sad little note:

"Dear Son,

I send three bearers to see you and bring me word how ye do, and to remember you that ye have in me a loving mother that wishes you to learn in time, to love, know and fear God."

But, on the orders of Elizabeth, paranoid about secret missives which could have been somehow concealed, being sent by Mary to her son, neither the pony nor the letter were allowed to cross the border.[21]

That night in his bedchamber, whither they had departed to discuss private matters, perhaps over a flagon of wine, Moray asked his guests to join him in Edinburgh where, on the following Monday or Tuesday, he was due to meet certain Scottish nobles to debate the problem of English rebels. On the Saturday he sent messengers to the Earls of Morton and Lindsay and the border magnate Lord Home, to join him in Edinburgh, which he hoped his English guests would attend.

Moray himself, for some reason was then delayed, so that it was only on Tuesday 22nd, that he left Stirling to ride to Edinburgh. The Hamiltons, informed of this happening, were waiting for him, tracking him all the way. Due to the early darkness of January Moray spent the night in Linlithgow, before rising early to continue to Edinburgh the next day.

Moray had been warned of danger lurking in Linlithgow, although he may have been unaware that Archbishop Hamilton had a house in the town overlooking the main street. Certainly he could not have guessed that on the fore-stair of that building, hidden by flapping linen sheets hung out to dry, lurked Hamilton of Bothwellhaugh with "a fyrlock chargt with two balls," levelled so accurately that, as the Regent, believing "that by ryding quicklie through the toune, being guarded by multitudes," that they could hardly single him out amongst the rest, galloped down the street, "he shot him with one ball, under the navell quite through."

Then, without waiting to see what had happened, but hearing screams from the street, Hamilton slipped out of the back of the house into the yard where his horse was waiting. Then suddenly, he realised that the back door of the yard was so low that his large horse, which must have been led in from the front, could not get under it. Fortunately, the wall above the door-head was only built of dry stone, which, frantic in his haste, he pulled down with his bare scrabbling hands. Then jumping on to the huge beast he was away only just in time, for he heard the sound of shouts and running feet behind him even as he galloped away from the scene of his crime. Behind him the thud of hoof-beats pursuing grew louder. He spurred his horse still harder until, seeing a wide ditch full of water in front of him, he pulled his dagger from his belt and struck the animal across the haunches so that, stung by both pain and terror, it cleared the ditch in one enormous leap. Thus Hamilton of Bothwellhaugh got away to the safe haven of Hamilton, duthus of his family's lands.

Meanwhile, back in Linlithgow, Moray had dismounted and walked back to the lodging he had only just left. Surgeons were quickly summoned, who at first thought the wound curable but then, as the bleeding continued, knew that he could not survive. So, on the same night, died the man known throughout Scotland as 'The Good Regent.' Moray was the half-brother of Queen Mary, who but for the illegitimacy of his birth should himself had been King of Scotland. In many ways he had failed the sister, whose throne he had aimed at himself, but for all that had faithfully served her son, the little nephew, whom he had left at Stirling Castle only the previous day. Mercifully, because of his youth and the coldness of the time of year, James was not taken to the funeral when Moray was buried in St Giles Cathedral in Edinburgh where John Knox preached the sermon on the text "Blessed are the dead which die in the Lord." [22]

CHAPTER 8
The Grandfather

Moray was dead and who could succeed him? Queen Elizabeth in England had her own ideas. Elizabeth had just been excommunicated by the Pope, which left her vulnerable to an invasion, by either or both of the Catholic countries of France and Spain, to avenge what they termed her heresy. For this reason she professed to be planning, at some future unspecified date, to reinstate her captive cousin, the Catholic Mary Queen of Scots, to her Scottish throne, hoping thereby to at least in some part conciliate the leaders of the enemies now threatening invasion from abroad.

At the same time, her real wish was to support the strength of the young King James. Who better to do so than his grandfather, the now ageing Matthew, Earl of Lennox, father of Mary's husband Darnley who, like so many others, believed that his son had been murdered through Mary's connivance if not actually at her command. Despite his being nominally a Catholic, the lords of the King's party were willing to accept Lennox in knowledge of his detestation of the daughter-in-law who, despite her acquittal at an English court, he still held responsible for the death of his beloved Henry.

Immediately, following Darnley's death, some of Queen Mary's supporters in Scotland had raided the north of England, thus unwittingly playing into Queen Elizabeth's hands. It gave a very real excuse for her to despatch an army, under the Earl of Sussex, to retaliate with similar destruction. Subsequently, she ordered Lennox, whose wife, the former Lady Margaret Douglas, half-sister of James V, and their surviving son Charles, were her dependents for their English lands, to proceed to Scotland without delay.

Matthew Lennox accompanied Sussex to the fortified town of Berwick-on-Tweed. Thither went Sir James Melville, sent by the lords who comprised the King's party, to discover from Sussex what his intentions were and whose side he supported, the exiled Queen's or her son's? Melville got on famously with Sussex, who paid all his expenses and even lent him his own night-gown 'furred with rich furrings.' Sussex assured him that he was impartial to the warring forces in Scotland but he did say privately that he thought that on Queen Elizabeth's demise, both Queen Mary and her son were indisputably heirs to the crown of England. He also revealed that he knew of the old and bitter feud between the houses of Lennox and Hamilton and had been deliberately, "directed secretly to kindle a fire of discord between two strong factions in Scotland, which could not be easily quenched."

Then being in Berwick, "when the Earl of Lennox was so far forward to be regent, I thought it my duty to visit him." Lennox was apparently most grateful, telling Melville that he had been so long away in England that he did not know of how things stood. Melville, having described how the situation between the parties adhering to the Queen and her son had resulted in civil war, strongly advised Lennox from taking on the 'regiment' as he called the government in Edinburgh, at that time held for the King, for should he attempt to do so he would almost certainly be killed.

According to one source Lennox, on reaching Berwick, had summoned men from his own district in the west of Scotland to escort him to Edinburgh. In April 1570, his land agent and general factotum, John Cunningham of Drumquhassle, is claimed to have led the English army to Edinburgh. [23] More specifically the records of the Scottish parliament prove that, in July 1570, Drumquhassle was appointed as Collector General for a special tax to be levied to raise funds to send ambassadors to England. [24] The hitherto inconsequential laird from west Stirlingshire was now plainly a man of some note.

Despite Melville's warning, Lennox, when he reached Edinburgh, did accept to head the government. His first action was to take the Angus town of Brechin, held by some companies of foot soldiers, most of whom fled from his arrival while some, taking refuge in the kirk and steeple, were all seized and summarily hanged. This accomplished, he took the Perthshire town of Doune, before heading for Dumbarton where the castle, place of his birth and main fortress of the Lennox, was held by Lord Fleming for the Queen.

Sadly, it was at this point that Sir William Kirkaldy of Grange, who had succeeded Sir James Balfour as governor of Edinburgh Castle, a great friend of Lennox's when the two had been together in France, quarrelled with the heads of the King's party and believing her to be the rightful sovereign of Scotland, joined with the Queen's. Delighted to hear this, the English ambassador, reported to the court of England that 'he had kindled a fire in Scotland that could not be easily extinguished.'

Meanwhile, Lennox had found a soldier of fortune, a Captain Thomas Crawford of Jordanhill, who was willing to try to storm Dumbarton Castle with a party of hand-picked men. Supporting them was Lennox's own contingent, mostly farm workers on the land, to which his factor, John Cunningham of Drumquhassle had sent out the fiery cross to summon them to assemble at given points from where he would lead them to join Crawford, acting as his second in command.

But, it was Lennox himself who, from the days of his childhood clambering about on the castle walls, could tell Thomas Crawford that on one side of the curtain wall, the rock below forming the castle's foundation, was so precipitous that the sentries thought it unnecessary to man it because no one in their senses would attempt such a suicidal climb. Lennox, even after what must have been almost fifty years, clearly remembered a sapling, left to grow in a crevice of the rock, which, if now as was probable had grown into a tree, would form a convenient hand-hold.

It seemed that luck favoured him. Even the weather complied, as in a thick fog, driven in from the sea, Crawford, Drumquhassle and their men, using very unstable ladders, climbed up the rock as Lennox had directed and clambered over the parapet wall. From there they turned the guns of the nearest batteries on the guards who, totally disordered in surprise, surrendered to save their own lives.

Not so fortunate was Archbishop Hamilton, a visitor to the castle, who was promptly arrested and imprisoned in the dungeon from which it was almost impossible to escape. Lennox was openly delighted that Hamilton, the illegitimate brother of the Earl of Arran (made Duke of Châtelhérault by the King of France), cleverest and most influential of the family, whom he had such good reason to hate, was now a helpless captive in his hands. Taken to Stirling, charged with the murder of Darnley, in which crime he had certainly been involved, he was hanged on 7 April 1751, his body then being drawn and quartered in the terrible execution that was still so frequently enacted in sixteenth century times.[25]

For Lennox the capture of Dumbarton Castle, chief bastion of his family's domains, was a triumph in which he rejoiced. Rewarded for the part he had played in its liberation, his factor, Cunningham of Drumquhassle, already high in his favour, was made captain of the great fortress placed so strategically to guard the entrance to the Clyde. Likewise, held high in the estimation of other men of influence, it was thanks to his cousin, Lord Mar, captain or governor of Stirling Castle, that Drumquhassle obtained the even more prestigious appointment of Master of the Royal Household of the young King James.[26]

John Cunningham of Drumquhassle, in his new position, received payment from the Treasurer of Scotland. But like all favourites he had enemies, men who, calling him a sycophant, resented the rise to eminence of this hitherto unimportant Stirlingshire laird. Scoffed at as a parvenu, who, on the word of Melville had only self-advancement in mind, his enemies brought a case against both him and his son-in-law, a neighbouring landlord Douglas of Mains, (Milngavie today) charging them with some action during the recent campaign. But thanks to their standing with the Regent Lennox, both were discharged by an act of parliament of any form of crime. [27]

James was five when, in August 1571, he made his first official appearance. A convention of Estates was held in Stirling and while the Honours of Scotland were still in Edinburgh Castle, the King was brought to the ceremony wearing a royal robe and with a small substitute crown and a sword and sceptre carried before him. A throne had been made for him at the head of the Great Hall, below which, as he stood on the steps beside his grandfather, he made a carefully rehearsed, short speech.

"My lords and other true subjects, we are converged here as I understand to do justice, and because my age will not suffer me to do my charge myself, I have given my power to my Godsire as regent, and, to do; and you will answer to God and me hereafter."[28]

This was followed by a speech from the Regent, while the King sat fidgeting as was only natural for a child. Then suddenly diverted, as he looked up and saw a hole in the ceiling where obviously a slate was missing, he piped up, "I think there is ane holl in this parliament."

A shocked silence followed. Whereas today everyone would have laughed, then it was a bad omen, which stuck in the assembled men's minds.

As this was happening, the Queen's party, at the instigation of Kirkaldy of Grange and Mary's secretary Maitland of Lethington, who had taken refuge in Edinburgh Castle, were holding a rival parliament. Kirkaldy of Grange was the one who decided to spring a surprise attack on Stirling, where it was known that precautions against such a happening were very slack. The plan was to take as many prisoners as possible and to bring them back to Edinburgh where they would be forced to join the Queen's party on the terms dictated to them by its leaders.

Grange wanted to lead the attack himself but those closest to him persuaded him against it on the grounds that his own life was too valuable to their cause to be hazarded in an enterprise involving so much risk. As it was, he watched the party of armed men ride off with great misgivings on the evening of 3 September. With them they took many spare horses, gathered from the market and elsewhere, to carry their intended prisoners back to Edinburgh.

Having ridden all night by the light of flaming torches, the assailants reached Stirling just as dawn was breaking over the town, so easily recognisable by the outline of the castle standing dominant against the lightening sky. Admitted by a townsman, committed to their cause, through a door into a little passage, they burst into the streets with cries of, "A Hamilton! A Hamilton! Remember the Archbishop who is to be avenged."

The King's lords, woken by the shouting and trampling of horses' feet staggered from their lodgings, pulling on clothes and armour and seizing weapons as they went. Amongst them Glencairn, Eglinton, Cassilis and Ruthven, surrendered without a fight. Lennox, knowing what likely fate awaited him, stayed within doors as long as he could, until persuaded by his servants that he had no means to resist the enemies now thronging the streets. Coming out of his lodging eventually, he surrendered himself to the laird of Wormeston, on the promise that his life would be spared.

The Earl of Morton refused to move until the roof of the house he occupied was burning over his head. Forced out by smoke, he surrendered to Sir Walter Scott of Buccleugh. But by then the King's men had gained a respite as some of the rebels deserted, intent on looting the merchants' stalls in the town, while up at the Castle the garrison heard the call to arms.

The Earl of Mar, with a party of harquebusiers, led the downhill charge. Many of the townsmen joined him, scattering the attackers, some of them clutching purloined goods, who, realising that they were defeated, fled, jostling each other at the city gate as they tried to get through to where the horses, saddled to carry the prisoners back to Edinburgh, were waiting beyond the walls.

The Regent Lennox was sitting behind the laird of Wormeston, who had promised to save him, astride the same horse. They were actually outside the town gates when a man called Captain Calder, on the order of Lord Claud Hamilton, shot the Regent with such precision that the bullet, which fatally wounded him, went through Wormeston's body as well.

Wormeston either fell, or was lifted from the horse, on which the Regent, slumped in the saddle, supported by men on either side, was taken back into the town and up the long steep road to the Castle, for him an agonising ride. Passing under the portcullis, he was carried into the courtyard from where a doorway led to the royal apartments. Such was the commotion, as the bearers shouted for a surgeon to be brought, that few even noticed the small, frightened, wide-eyed boy, who stood watching the grandfather he had learned to love, being carried past him with blood dripping from his wound.

Yet Lennox's thoughts were for him, "If the bairn be well, all is well," were almost the last dying words of the man plagued with guilt over the hanging of boy hostages, while fighting for King Henry, now so long ago in Carlisle. From the bed where they laid him, he sent for the King's lords, to whom he was clear-minded enough to give instructions, telling them to seek the peace, to support the King, his little grandson, and to appoint a trustworthy regent, indicating the man whose hand he gripped in his agony, the Earl of Mar. It was to him that he gave a last message of farewell to his "dearest Madge," as he called his formidable wife, to whom he had remained devoted after a marriage of many years. He then asked all around him to pray for him which, although they were not Catholics, they did until he died that same afternoon.

James would never forget the horror and shock of the happenings on that August day when he was only five years old. Later his revulsion at the sight of blood, believed by some to have resulted from his near death experience in his mother's womb, was in fact more naturally related to what, as a sensitive child, he had been forced to watch so unwillingly and retain in his bewildered mind.

CHAPTER 9
The Third Regent

Following the death of the Earl of Lennox there were three candidates for the regency, the Earl of Morton, the Earl of Argyll and the Earl of Mar. Eventually, as Lennox had hoped, it was Mar who was chosen by the Convention of Estates and proclaimed regent at the Mercat Cross in Stirling. Already governor of Stirling Castle, and guardian to the young King, Mar was elected for his quality of leadership and proven integrity. Although of a peace-loving nature, he did not shrink from contention when it came to attempting to take the city of Edinburgh and the castle, of which he had been a former governor, by now held by Kirkaldy of Grange, most loyal supporter of the Queen.

The civil war continued, the King's party being based at Leith, while Grange, with the great cannons lodged, not only in the castle, but in St Giles' Churchyard and at Kirk O'Field, was defending both the castle and the city within the walls. An attempt to take Edinburgh by assault failed and Mar then continued what became known as 'The Lang Siege.' Neither side took prisoners nor did hideous cruelty result as seems inevitable in civil war. Mar himself finally withdrew to Stirling saying, as Melville quoted, that, "he could see nothing but the wreck of the country, under pretext of owning the King's and Queen's authority, while neither was in any of their minds, but they were pushed only by their own partialities of ambition, greediness and vengeance, England kindling up both parties and then laughing them all to scorn."[29]

Mar's appointment as regent certainly did not please Queen Elizabeth, who would like to have seen the Earl of Morton in his place. Disappointed in Randolph, whose duplicity in favouring Morton had been revealed, she sent a new ambassador to

Scotland, a Mr Henry Killigrew, an old friend of Melville's to take his place. Killigrew arrived, presumably by ship landing at Leith, before setting off for Stirling. Hearing that Melville had just crossed the Firth of Forth from Fife, he sent a message to Edinburgh Castle to see if by any chance he was there. He was and they met at Crammond, where Killigrew said he came with a commission to try and settle the discord between both parties. He added that the Queen and council of England had no high regard for the Earl of Mar, but pinned all their hopes on the Earl of Morton, whom they knew had a great following in Scotland and whom, for this reason, they thought should be regent instead of Mar.

Shortly after this Melville had a letter from Mar himself, asking him to come to him. He did so and was forced to listen to what he called 'a great moan' of the civil troubles that were kindled in Scotland by the craft and malice of people both in Scotland and England. Mar then asked him to go to Edinburgh to show them, "how that we are led upon the ice, and that all good Scotsmen would fain agree and settle the state…Whereupon I went to Edinburgh, and found them all inclined to peace and quietness, with little need of persuasion thereto, for they were near a point before with my Lord of Lennox."

But then in August 1572 came catastrophe, as the dreadful news of the Massacre of St Bartholomew's day circulated round Scotland. People reacted in horror on hearing that an estimated 3,000 Huguenots had been slaughtered in Paris, many of them drowned by Catholics in the River Loire. Such was the publicity that Protestants in all parts of Europe began to believe it to be only the start of a purge by vengeful Catholics to exterminate them everywhere. No one was safe. In Scotland and England there was a general surge of belief that Mary Stuart, figurehead of a probable Catholic revolution, must die.

On the strength of the public terror in both countries, Queen Elizabeth entered into negotiation with the Earl of Mar to hand Queen Mary over to him to be executed in Scotland. Mar, to his eternal discredit, initially played along with her, but insisted that if Elizabeth wanted to forward her cousin's execution, she must do so publicly. "Mary Stuart," he told her, "must be brought from her English prison to Scotland by English soldiers, together with a chosen representative, who must be present at the execution."

Elizabeth was in fact stalling, unwilling to accept responsibility for Mary's death as was Mar himself. Negotiations dragged on, nothing being settled until, on 28 October, they came to a sudden halt as Mar died under very suspicious circumstances.

The Regent, it had been noticed, had become very tired and ill. Greatly depressed by the awful decisions he was being asked to make, forced upon him by circumstances hitherto unseen. He had not aimed for the regency but had accepted it out of duty to the King, whom he most loyally served. Now he was being asked to order the death of that King's mother to whom, but a few years previously, he had sworn loyalty, as Scotland's anointed Queen.

Overcome by the load of anxiety, which would have proved a heavy burden even to a much younger man, he was seen to be failing physically. Sir James Melville, describing how until the very end Mar had continued to try and effect some form of peace which might avoid the execution of Queen Mary, wrote:

"The Regent went to Edinburgh to convene the lords of the council, to show them the calamities that the civil war produced, and to let them see how necessary agreement and a settled state would be to the whole country. In the meantime, until the appointed council-day, he went to Dalkeith, where he was nobly treated and banqueted by the Lord of Morton, shortly after which he took a vehement sickness, which caused him to ride suddenly to Stirling, where he died, regretted by many. Some of his friends and the vulgar people spoke and suspected he had gotten wrong, and others that it was for displeasure."[30]

Inevitably there were rumours of poison. Arsenic in powder form was so easy to scatter over a dish of spiced meat or even a salad as Lord Leicester, apparently a practised poisoner, is accused of having done. Melville does not mention it directly, perhaps afraid to do so for fear of repercussion, or because he believed, as did many others at the time, that Mar had literally been killed by the work load, which, through a sense of duty, he had felt himself bound to undertake.

However mistrusted, it was Morton who became regent following the death of the Earl of Mar. James Douglas, Earl of Morton, was the second son of Sir George Douglas of

Pittendreich, who, as the heir to his brother, the 6th Earl of Angus, (with no surviving son) was known as the Master of Douglas. Sir George Douglas, had married a kinswoman, Elizabeth, daughter and heiress of David Douglas of Pittendreich near Elgin, who was the legal representative of the 3rd Earl of Morton, whose lands were at that time forfeited to the crown. However, when the Douglasses had been reinstated in 1543, Sir George had married his second son James to Morton's youngest daughter, called Elizabeth after her mother. Sadly, probably due to their over-close relationship, Elizabeth and both of her elder sisters, one of whom married the 2nd Earl of Arran and the other Lord Maxwell, were all insane. Nonetheless, it was through his marriage to the mad Elizabeth that, on the death of her father in 1553, James Douglas became the Earl of Morton as the 4th Earl.

By 1563 he had been made Lord Chancellor of Scotland. Two years later it was he who had headed the armed force, which had entered Holyrood Palace to murder David Rizzio and it was to his house that the conspirators had afterwards gathered at. But it was not for the killing of Queen Mary's unfortunate Italian secretary, but as the main instigator in the assassination of her husband, Henry Darnley, that Morton was to later to stand trial.

Born in 1516, Morton was already nearly sixty when made regent in 1577. After this in 1573, he had achieved what previous regents had failed to do, by reaching an agreement with the Hamiltons. In February, the Duke of Châtelhérault, as thanks to his French title the 2nd Earl of Arran was now known, gave his assent to the Pacification of Perth, which ended the war between the Catholic supporters of Mary Queen of Scots and the Protestant lords who had forced her abdication in favour of her son James VI. Queen Mary's supporters agreed to recognise Morton as regent in return for a full pardon and restoration of their forfeited lands.

But while the 'Pacification' granted a general pardon for all who had fought against the King's party in the civil war, it excluded anyone known to have been involved in the murders of the Regents Moray and Lennox. The Lords John and Claud Hamilton, sons of the Duke of Châtelhérault, were accused but escaped death by flight, Lord John going to France and his brother to England to be given sanctuary by Queen Elizabeth at her court. Nonetheless their estates were forfeited as Morton enacted his revenge on the family he still regarded as the greatest challenge to his power.

Yet in Edinburgh Castle, the Queen's most faithful champion, William Kirkaldy, laird of Grange, still held out for the imprisoned Queen Mary, betrayed by those who had sworn to serve her, as he believed. Hoping that help would come from France, Kirkaldy defied the people of Edinburgh, who had rebelled against him after he had set some of their houses on fire and had turned the guns against them as they had tried to extinguish the flames. Barricading himself in the castle he waited for the inevitable attack.

It came on 2 May 1573 when Sir William Drury, the Marshal and Deputy Governor of Berwick-on-Tweed, led an English army within gun-shot of the walls. A cannonade then started, causing dreadful casualties on both sides.

"Theire was a verey grate slaughter amongst the English canoniers, sundries of them having their legges and armes torne from ther bodies in the aire by the violence of the grate shote," as the diarist Robert Birrel reported.

Kirkaldy hung on, still clinging to the hope of a miracle in the form of French relief. But it did not come and in the dry summer weather the castle well ran dry. Men were lowered by ropes to bring water from the nearby St Margaret's Well but the water was poisoned, it was claimed, on the orders of Morton, so that at last, on 29 May, the man who had risked all for Queen Mary was forced to surrender. Maitland of Lethington, the Queen's former secretary, who had been with him, had taken refuge in a cellar in Leith where he died, either from the paralytic disease from which he had been suffering, or, as many people claimed, by his own hand. Kirkaldy of Grange, imprisoned and charged as a traitor, was hanged at the Mercat Cross in Edinburgh, a hero to the public mind.

CHAPTER 10
The Fourth Regent

Following the death of the Earl of Mar, his brother, Alexander, the Master of Erskine, together with his mother, the redoubtable Annabella, became guardians of the young King. His tutors were still George Buchanan and Peter Young, while John Cunningham, the laird of Drumquhassle remained Master of the Household. In addition the Abbots of Cambuskenneth and Dryburgh, both of them Erskines and laymen who held the abbey property, taught the boy King to ride horses, at which, when once in the saddle, unencumbered by the disability of his deformed foot, he soon became adept. Also, once an accomplished horseman, he learnt the skills of hunting and hawking, both sports which throughout his lifetime he is known to have so passionately enjoyed.

But the new regent Morton had many enemies. Buchanan, with whom he had quarrelled over a horse, which he borrowed and refused to return, being one. Another was the laird of Drumquhassle, furious because Morton kept all casualties (the property and revenue usually pertaining to the crown, through the feudal system of land tenure and proceedings through the courts of law) for himself.

Drumquhassle was not the only one to resent him on this account. So great was the feeling against Morton that a friend, a Mr Nichol Elphinston, warning that many wished to destroy him, advised him to try to placate at least some of them with monetary bribes. This he proceeded to do, giving as Melville reported, "to one that was of mean rank twenty pieces of gold, at twenty pounds the piece." But still the feeling against Morton increased with unstoppable force. Foremost amongst his enemies was James's great uncle, he who in the parish kirk of Stirling had crowned him when he was just thirteen months old. Robert

Stuart, Bishop of Orkney, brother of James's grandfather the late Regent Lennox with whom he had escaped to England, now openly accused the regent of some underhanded dealing with Denmark.

Then came a newcomer to the court, the handsome, charming, quick-witted James Stewart, a younger son of Lord Ochiltree, a soldier of fortune who soon had King James, who admired him immensely, under his thrall. Stewart, like the bishop, filled the boy's head with suspicions of crime against Morton and James was only too ready to believe them, distrusting the regent as he did.

Morton's cousin, Sir William Douglas of Lochleven, half-brother of the late Regent Moray, was another who warned James of the danger in which he stood.

"I pray your grace flatter not yourself, for if your Grace believes that ye have the goodwillers, ye deceive yourself" and Nichol Elphinston further assured him that the new regent [Morton] was intent on increasing not only his power, but his wealth, ostensibly through the auspices of the Crown.

It was due to this undisguised ambition that Morton made such bitter enemies of the Earl and Countess of Argyll. Colin Campbell, 6th Earl of Argyll, had married Agnes Keith, widow of the Regent Moray and she was now the custodian of the superb collection of jewels that Queen Mary, while imprisoned in the castle of Lochleven had entrusted to her half-brother, the Earl of Moray. Particularly valuable and of great sentimental importance was the great jewel, in the form of the letter H. Set with diamonds, which had been given to Mary by her first father-in-law, Henri II of France. This, together with the other jewels, the Countess refused to part, appealing both to the Scottish Parliament and to Queen Elizabeth to be allowed to keep them which, as she believed, was her right. But Morton over-ruled them, putting both the Countess and her husband to the horn as rebels, until she eventually released to him three great rubies and nine great diamonds as well as the much coveted broach in the form of an H, the present from the French King. In addition to this, anyone who had fought for the Queen's party, defunct since the capture of Edinburgh Castle and the death of Kirkaldy of Grange, was now forced by Morton to pay heavy fines. Still more in proof of his arrogance, he had himself made collector of the thirds of benefices, exacted by the Crown, from the teinds of the Kirk.

In September 1577, Morton attended a meeting of the Privy Council in Stirling attended by the twelve year-old King. Also there were the young Earl of Mar, the two abbots who were the King's preceptors, the Lord Ruthven and others. They passed an act declaring that the King, in future, should be, "served and attended upon in his Chamber with men, committing the care thereof to Alexander Erskine of Gogar, Master of Mar."[31]

Morton, it seemed, was unaware, that in agreeing to this he was permitting the King to be permanently in the care of men keen to displace him.

He was also oblivious to the fact, that by this time, the Earl of Argyll had become such a personal friend of King James that he had been given his own room in Stirling Castle to stay in whenever he wished. Meanwhile Argyll had made up a personal quarrel with the Earl of Atholl, described as 'a man of upright character' and the two had united against Morton whose dominance they greatly resented.

Argyll used his friendship with the King to lay before him his case against the Regent. But it was Drumquhassle, still Master of the Household, who, with the consent of both George Buchanan and the Master of Mar, as Melville puts it, 'secretly practised' the Earls of Argyll and Atholl to come to Stirling to attend a meeting officially summoned by the King, to which the rest of Morton's enemies also came.

Morton himself was summoned but, warned of what was happening, declined. Instead he sent evidence, taken by Lord Ruthven, one of his few remaining friends, of the Privy Council's actions against Argyll and Atholl, saying that if his Majestie saw fit to oversee their disobedience, that he would be pleased to resign his office."

The two Earls, with such explosive material in their hands, begged the King to accept Morton's resignation and take over the government himself. James was delighted. On 12 March 1578, his 'acceptance of the government' was proclaimed by a herald at the Mercat Cross in Edinburgh. Morton then appeared and publicly resigned his office. It seemed that *a fait accompli* had been achieved.

Apparently accepting the situation with good will, Morton then retired, not to his own castle of Dalkeith, but to that of his cousin, Sir William Douglas, on the island in Lochleven, from where, thirty years ago, Queen Mary had escaped to England.

There he kept himself occupied by making walks in the garden, while, as Sir James Melville wrote, his mind was occupied, "in crooked paths, with a complot how to be brought again to be master of the court, which was accomplished upon a night at midnight."[32]

It was some six weeks after Morton's resignation, towards the end of April, when the young Earl of Mar went to Stirling Castle to visit his uncle, the Master of Mar, still officially, the guardian of the King. A hunting expedition was planned. Very early in the morning of 26 April, the sportsmen were gathering in the Great hall, unaware that a few hours earlier, at midnight, the two abbots of Cambuskenneth and Dryburgh had secretly opened a door of the castle to allow Morton to quietly enter and hide in some undiscovered place.

Upstairs, in the Great Hall, the now ageing Alexander, Master of Mar, had risen to join the hunters, who included his nephew, the young earl, and the two abbots who had just so treacherously allowed Morton into the castle only a few hours before. Suddenly the Master found himself cornered by men, headed by the abbots, demanding the keys of the castle, of wronging his nephew and of holding the King by force. Still agile and quick thinking, despite his age, he grabbed a halberd from one of the guards and levelled its point at the Abbot of Dryburgh, loudly yelling for help. As men rushed to join him they met the weapons of those of the abbot's men in what turned into a wild stampede. Someone slipped and fell, trampled by heavy feet.

Then the Earl of Argyll appeared, drawn by the noise from his room, followed, for the same reason, by the young King. Terrified, James screamed as he saw the man, whom he thought to be the Master of Mar, killed by the pounding feet, lying helpless on the floor. Several were in fact dead but it was not the Master whom the king, now hysterical, was sobbing for, but his son. Found in fact to be still alive, but terribly injured, he died the following day.

Argyll and the Master, had managed to escape from the castle but returned to talk with the latter's nephew, the young

Earl of Mar and the two abbots, once the commotion died down. The Master resigned the charge of both the King and the castle to his nephew to be given the governorship of Edinburgh Castle in compensation. Argyll returned to his own country to raise his men in arms while Sir William Douglas, appearing later in the day, hastened back to Lochleven to tell Morton that the day was won.

Morton, triumphant, rode at once to Stirling to establish a firm hold over the King, who was still enduring nightmares, remaining in a highly nervous state. Nevertheless, on Morton's orders, he summoned a parliament to meet in the Great Hall of Stirling Castle, where the bloodstains had just been washed away. A new Privy Council was formed, with Morton as its First Lord, his dependents in the majority of those holding office.

Meanwhile Argyll and Atholl were raising an army in the King's name. Marching towards Stirling from Falkirk, they carried a banner embroidered with a boy looking out of a window and with the words

Liberty I crave
And cannot it have,
Either you shall have it
Or we will die for it.

At the same time Morton marched from Stirling and the two armies met somewhere half-way. Evenly matched, they prepared to fight, when the new English ambassador, the lawyer Robert Bowes, appeared and induced them to make a truce until the following May. Following this. Both Atholl and Argyll contrived to work peaceably with Morton as fellow councillors. Then on 16 April 1579, to celebrate the end of their enmity and conciliate on-going harmony, Morton held a great banquet at Stirling to which came all his allies and former enemies as well.

But Atholl left the banquet, plainly feeling ill. He managed to reach Kincardine and the house of the Earl of Montrose where, eight days later he died.

Poison was again suspected. It was too much of a coincidence that Atholl should die in the same way as had Mar after a similar banquet at Dalkeith Castle given by the same host. Morton was known to have been the instigator of the murder of

Darnley, Queen Mary's husband. It would seem that he would stop at nothing to gain his own ends.

Morton hotly denied the rumours casting foul aspersions at his name. Two of those, spreading them in rhyming lampoons, he caught and hanged but he could not prevent the Countess of Atholl's insistence in holding a post mortem. The corpse was dissected by several doctors all of whom agreed on the presence of poison with the exception of one, a Doctor Preston, highly esteemed in his profession, who licked the contents of the stomach after which he himself nearly died.[33]

King James was frankly terrified, believing that he would be the next to be killed. There was no halting to Morton's ambition. Plainly he would poison or murder anyone who attempted to limit his power. He did not even have the presence of the Master of Mar to console him. Mar had left the court ill with grief over the death of his son.

But Morton's enemies were plotting against him. Led by John Cunningham of Drumquhassle, they were seeking a replacement for the Earl of Atholl who would be pleasing, not only to the susceptible King, but to those still loyal to his mother, Queen Mary. There was one obvious candidate, whose birth, religion and known personal attraction, fitted all the categories that the enemies of Morton desired.

CHAPTER 11
The King's Great Love

It was Drumquhassle who, by tactfully reminding James of his cousin, Esmé Stuart, set in motion the coming from France to Scotland of this charismatic man. No one about the court, let alone Drumquhassle himself, could possibly have guessed at the overpowering strength of character of this relation who would so soon undermine the puritanical principles drummed into James by his tutors.

Esmé, was the son of John Stewart, 5th Lord Aubigny, the younger brother of James' grandfather Matthew Stewart, 4th Earl of Lennox, he who when regent, had been murdered so horribly in front of the five year old boy's eyes,

James took the bait immediately, leaping at the wonderful idea of inviting Esmé, who had been born and brought up in France, to come and visit him. His fear and depression, over recent happenings, seemed forgotten in excitement over the project, which Drumquhassle had put into his mind.

Esmé Stuart, born in 1542, had married Catherine de Balsac with whom at the time of his arrival in Scotland he had four children, the fifth a girl, who would later become the Countess of Mar, being yet to be born.

He was thirty-seven, twenty-five years older than James, when on 8 September 1579, he landed at Leith. With him came an entourage of French courtiers who, after being warmly welcomed by some prominent citizens of Edinburgh, then seized on the chance to accompany the visitors to Stirling. There, on the morning of the 15th, the King received them in the Great Hall of Stirling Castle. Sir James Melville, described d'Aubigny as "upright, just and gentle" and according to Bishop Spottiswoode, although he spoke only French and learned but a few Scottish words, "his courteous and modest behaviour" quickly won him friends and admirers.

As for James he was besotted, totally captivated by this tall, auburn-haired, red-bearded cousin, with the flashing black eyes of the Italian Vincentis, from whom he was descended. It has been suggested that, had d'Aubigny been female, his presence would have had the same effect. Lonely and starved of affection in his childhood, James simply wanted to be loved. As it was his passion for his dashing French cousin began his predilection for homosexual affairs.

D'Aubigny began by telling James that his visit would be a brief one, he had only come to congratulate him upon his, 'entrie to his Kingdome.' Shortly he must return home. James would have none of it. Nothing would do but that this new found relation should go with him to Edinburgh and join in the triumphal pageant that was being planned. D'Aubigny gave in with grace and on 28 September the court left Stirling to begin the triumphal progress to Edinburgh to celebrate the King, now just thirteen, taking over the government of Scotland to rule in his own name.

With them rode a great cavalcade of nobles, Morton and his nephew the Earl of Angus, Argyll, Montrose, the young John, Earl of Mar and d'Aubigny's French entourage amongst them, with an escort of 2,000 horsemen, following behind. At Corstorphine they were joined by the great Border families of the Humes and the Kers, with 300 armed men. As they neared the city of Edinburgh, a cannonade thundered out in welcome from the castle, while lustily the citizens cheered. But the capital city was not yet ready to receive him, preparations being still incomplete. So James made his way to Holyrood Palace, while the guns on the ships lying at Leith fired volleys of shots in his honour. [34]

On 17 October the King rode in procession into Edinburgh. Sitting astride his beautifully caparisoned horse, wearing a suit of white satin embroidered with silver, he made a splendid sight for the many spectators applauding him as he came. Reaching the West Port he was received by the magistrates of the town, standing below a canopy of purple velvet, who presented him with the sceptre and the sword of state and entertained him with a play of King Solomon, represented with two women who contended for the young child, a compliment to his own, by now well-known prestigious grasp of languages and learning.

He then rode up to the castle, his progress every now and then interrupted by more pageants and speeches of welcome.

As James returned towards Holyrood 'Dame Religion' emerged from St Giles, desiring his presence. Dismounting he entered the church to listen to a sermon before, once more astride his horse, in sharp and probably welcome contrast, he found Bacchus at the Mercat Cross distributing liquor to all and sundry. At the Netherbow he saw yet another pageant, this time of the planets which had shone in the sky at his birth and Ptolemaeus describing, "His beautie and fortune bestowed on him by the influence of the stares." Then on he went through streets, which rather strangely in October, are said to have been spread with flowers, as the people of Edinburgh shouted joyously in welcoming their young King, pushed and shoved to get a glimpse of him so, "that many were hurt in the streets through the throng."

Three days later, on 20 October, Parliament assembled with the King in charge. The forfeiture of the Hamilton lands was confirmed and amongst them, the rich Abbey of Arbroath, was granted to Esmé d'Aubigny, this being only the first of the honours to be heaped upon him by the infatuated King James.

Amongst those highly satisfied at the way in which proceedings were going, there was none more delighted than John Cunningham, the laird of Drumquhassle, whose own idea to bring the King's French cousin to Scotland had resulted in, what even to him, was an unexpected success. Pleased also was the King's other favourite, the dashing son of Lord Ochiltree, Captain James Stewart, "handsome and arrogant [who] thought no man his equal."

Stewart never lost an opportunity to spread malicious tales about Morton, mostly directed at the King's ear.

The Parliament once over it was generally assumed that James would return to Stirling Castle, where, with the Earl of Mar still the governor, the Erskines would have more control over his actions than in Edinburgh. But James had no intention of doing so, remaining instead at Holyrood where d'Aubigny occupied the best suite of rooms next to his own.

D'Aubigny had his own good reasons for staying, apart from his obvious enjoyment in being so well-entertained. James, as yet unmarried, had no direct heir. Charles Stuart, his uncle, his father Henry Darnley's younger brother, had died of tuberculosis three years before, leaving an only daughter, Arbella, born shortly before Charles's death, now a little fair-haired girl of five. Should she, for any reason fail to survive, Esmé d'Aubigny, as the grandson of James's grandfather, the Earl of Lennox's brother, would thus be directly in line to both the English and Scottish thrones.

Morton was highly suspicious of Esmé, believing him to have been sent by Queen Mary's French relations, the family of the Duc de Guise, to try to effect a Catholic rising in Scotland or England by which she might be freed. That this was not pure surmise was proved when the Scottish minister, Nicol Dagleish, was entertained in France by a staunchly Protestant Huguenot lady whose son, the Sieur de Monbirneau, a close friend of d'Aubigny, was one of the twenty companions with whom he had arrived in Scotland. This very holy lady had sent the Scottish minister home to warn the Presbyterian hierarchy of the danger of d'Aubigny's influence over the King.

Despite the calumnies spread by Morton, or perhaps due to the enmity between them, the Earl of Mar, firm Presbyterian that he was, now governor of Edinburgh Castle, seduced by the charm of d'Aubigny, became his friend. Likewise, he was joined by several leading Catholics and by Lord Seton, most faithful of the imprisoned Queen Mary's supporters in Scotland, together with Lord Ruthven, the Lord Treasurer, and the Commendator of Dunfermline, who was the Secretary of State. D'Aubigny's rise in influence seemed unstoppable, made more so when he converted to Protestantism to win over his enemies in the Kirk. James was so delighted that he persuaded his great uncle, Robert Stuart, the Bishop of Orkney, who following the death of both James' grandfather and the latter's grandson, had become the Earl of Lennox, to resign his title. Subsequently, on 5 March 1580, in Stirling Castle, James made Esmé d'Aubigny Earl of Lennox.

During the summer of 1580 James went on progress through the north of Scotland. Inevitably, d'Aubigny went with him, first to Perth, as the guest of Lord Ruthven, then on to Arbroath, where Lennox as the Commendator was his host. Then on to Dunottar, that castle sited on rocks above the North Sea in Aberdeenshire, home of the Earl Marischal who took them hunting stags (not in those days out of season) and feasted them with banquets at night. Then it was back to St Andrews for a Convention of Estates.

It was here that Morton joined them, still limping from the kick of a horse which had left him unable to walk. Morton was depressed, not only as the result of his injury, but because of warnings that, thanks to d'Aubigny's influence, the King mistrusted him. He would listen to no one else.

James, with his entourage, returned to Holyrood in September. D'Aubigny was then made, not only a Privy Councillor, First Gentleman of the bedchamber and Lord Chamberlain, but Governor of the Lennox family bastion of Dumbarton Castle.

The laird of Drumquhassle, erstwhile Governor of Dumbarton, was furious, no doubt cursing the day he had ever mentioned the name of his French cousin to the King. Now he found that d'Aubigny meant to demote him from captain to constable thus robbing him of the authority to pay or move soldiers of the garrison. The English ambassador, Sir Robert Bowes, reported to Sir Francis Walsingham, just made principal secretary to Queen Elizabeth that Drumquhassle had asked for his advice. Queen Elizabeth had instructed Bowes to tell Drumquhassle to hold on to Dumbarton Castle by any means possible, and upon letters to Drumquhassle from England being intercepted, the ports of Edinburgh, on the orders of d'Aubigny were closed, so that Drumquhassle could not seek help from across the border.

Instead, he was forced to deliver the castle to d'Aubigny, but was slightly mollified when compensated with a bond of £40,000 (Scots) for his compliance. Bowes then tried to pacify Queen Elizabeth by telling her that the Stirlingshire laird, "hath more wit than honesty." [35]

Esmé d'Aubigny, in his office of Lord Chamberlain, soon began to take command. Responsible for the King's safety, he immediately arranged that twenty-four gentlemen should attend on James, eight of them at a time. Over and above this he organised a guard of sixty soldiers, under the command of his ally, Captain James Stewart. The English ambassador Robert Bowes, acting on Queen Elizabeth's instructions, objected, saying that Lennox was nothing but an agent of the Guises. James, however, ignored him. Nothing that his favourite did was wrong. Morton's days were numbered. Lennox was already planning his doom.

On 30th December the King took Morton hunting, spending the day with him as though they were the greatest of friends. Morton however, was not deceived knowing that retribution waited in whatever form it took. He was not mistaken. At the Privy Council meeting the next day Captain James Stewart rushed into the chamber to fall on his knees before the King, pointing with one hand at Morton accusing him of causing Lord Darnley's, James' father's, death. Morton swung round towards the King and Lennox and calling Stewart the spokesman of his enemies, drew his sword. Stewart leapt up, pulling out his own weapon determined to kill. But Lord Cathcart and Lord Lindsay pulled the two men apart. Morton was imprisoned, first in Holyrood and then in Edinburgh Castle, from where he was taken to Dumbarton where he is claimed to have been badly treated and starved.

Queen Elizabeth was furious, sending Sir Thomas Randolph, her former ambassador to Scotland to demand Morton's fair trial. But the King would not listen to him, "he wants neither words nor answers to anything said to him." Randolph complained, before, after a pistol was fired by one of Morton's enemies through the window of the Provost of Edinburgh's house in which he was lodging, the English envoy fled to Berwick.

Back in England he told Queen Elizabeth, that while taught to give protestations of friendship to her, cousin King James was practising secretly with the Catholic States, whereupon another English noble endorsed this by saying that, "The King's fair speeches and promises, will fall out to be plain dissimulation, wherein his is in his tender years better practised than others forty years older than he is. He is holden among the Scots for the greatest dissembler that ever was heard of for years."

Told of Morton's ruin Elizabeth exclaimed, "That false Scotch urchin! What can be expected from the double dealing of such an urchin as this?"[36]

Randolph had already left Scotland before, at the end of May 1581, Morton was brought across Scotland to Edinburgh to be tried. His enemies, Argyll, Montrose and Maxwell were amongst the jurors, as well as Sir James Balfour, supposed to produce the famous Ainslie Bond, signed that night in Edinburgh by the men intending Darnley's death.

Sir James Balfour could not produce the vital paper—it has been suggested because he himself had signed it—but he did testify to Morton's being that of "Art and part" to the crime. Morton denied it strongly, but nonetheless, was condemned to be hanged, drawn and quartered the next day. The King, perhaps from a guilty conscience, commuted the sentence to beheading and Morton was executed by 'the Maiden' a form of guillotine which he himself had imported, on the morning of 2 June 1581. Standing beside the instrument of death, as the blade fell on Morton's neck, was Captain James Stewart, triumphant so it was reported, at the sight of his enemy's extinction.

Thus died the last of the four regents who, during James VI's minority, had ruled in his stead. Morton was certainly ruthless, not averse to poisoning his enemies if stories against him can be believed. But to his credit it must be remembered that he did end the civil war in Scotland to restore at least some form of order in a country torn apart by strife.

James was by now fifteen years old. With no time for music and dancing, the main entertainments of the court, he was happiest when hunting, always his favourite pursuit. Six pairs of thoroughbred horses, sent as a present from the Duke of Guise, entranced him and his skill in horsemanship was reported by the English ambassador Thomas Randolph. "Tuesday last," he wrote in 1581, "the King ran at the ring, and, for a child, did very well...The next day the King came to Edinburgh to the preaching. That afternoon he spent in like pastimes as he had done the day before." At Leith, where he dined a few days later, a castle built on boats and called in derision the Pope's palace, was bravely assaulted and set on fire. There was horse racing on the sands and a ludicrous joust between courtiers in small boats.

Innocent as these sports would seem to have been Sir James Melville was censorious of the company James kept. Gone was the influence of his tutors, Buchanan and even the gentler Peter Young, those strict Presbyterian men. Instead it was d'Aubigny and Arran, whose swearing and bawdy jokes, were to Melville's mind utterly obscene.

'It was a pity to see so well brought up a Prince thus miserably corrupted,' he wrote, 'both with evil and dangerous principles of government in Kirk and commonwealth. He was made to think evil of those who had served him best and to regard the Reformation as done by a privy section turbulently.'

Worse still, 'Arran put the opinion of absolute power in his Majesty's head,' and Patrick Adamson, the Bishop of St Andrews, taught him he should have bishops under him to hold the Kirk in order.[37]

Arran, as head of the Catholic faction in Scotland, did indeed use his power to ruin the leaders of the Protestant lords, namely Gowrie, Mar and those other allied to the Reformation established now twenty years ago. Amongst those singled out for punishment was the laird of Drumquhassle, who with his son-in-law, the Douglas Laird of Mains, together with others, on, March 1581 was accused, under Arran's direction, of being involved in a plot against d'Aubigny with the support of the English government. Some of the Scottish nobles had indeed been in the pay of England, including Drumquhassle, who had received a pension.

CHAPTER 12
The Favourite's Fall

D'Aubigny's next honour was to be made Lord of Dalkeith, the title, as well as the castle of that name, having been that of Morton. Further to this, on 5 August 1851, James made his cousin the Duke of Lennox.

At the same time the King's other favourite, James Stewart, the son of Lord Ochiltree and brother-in-law of John Knox, who had become captain of James's personal bodyguard, on the pretext of descent from a daughter of the first Hamilton Earl of Arran, on 22 April 1581, was advanced to the earldom of Arran (vacant since the forfeiture of the Hamiltons, the Duc de Châtelhérault and his sons). It was Stewart who, having stood on the steps of the scaffold, triumphant at Morton's death, had then abducted and married the Earl of March's wife, a lady avaricious as himself.

Stewart had been a friend of d'Aubigny to the point where the Frenchman, unused both to Scotland and its people, turned to him for advice. But from this time on, it would seem at his wife's instigation, he deliberately began misleading him, by making insinuations against his friends, a plan that worked successfully as d'Aubigny, believing Stewart's calumnies, lost his temper with several of them, turning them against him by his rage. Likewise, again at Stewart's prompting, the English ambassador Bowes stirred up people against the King's cousin on the old charge of his being a papist, acting as an agent of the Duke of Guise.

At the same time, even without Stewart's insinuations against them, many of the nobility of Scotland, began to see both d'Aubigny and Stewart as dangerous, their influence over the King a threat, not only to themselves but to possession of their land. If Morton could be disposed of, his titles and property so swiftly given away, who, if the favourites cast greedy eyes over their possessions, might be the next one to suffer a similar fate?

Meanwhile the newly made Earl of Arran, James Stewart, over-stepped the mark. Confident of his power over the King, he quarrelled fiercely with d'Aubigny, threatening to fight him in a duel. James was horrified. Esmé d'Aubigny was not only his cousin but also his nearest male heir. Moreover he loved him as the companion and confidante for whom he had so greatly longed. Suddenly his mind was clear–as he recognised Arran as the scheming adventurer that he was.

Arran's disgrace became plain when James, as his cousin's guest, went to Dalkeith Castle for the Christmas of 1581. Arran, specifically refused an invitation, was ordered not to attend. Then hardly were the festivities ended before, in January of the New Year, Arran's wife gave birth to a son, thus proving their adultery, for which the Kirk ordered them both to do public penance before the child could be christened under Presbyterian rights.

Worse was to follow. When the King, with Lennox, returned to Holyrood, he at once ordered Arran to be dismissed from the captaincy of the guard, giving it to Lennox in his place. Arran, now acutely aware of how he had over-played his hand, decided, through a third party, to seek conciliation with Lennox, which the Duke graciously accepted much to King James' delight. His two favourites were friends again. Nothing more could go wrong.

But it did. The conniving laird of Drumquhassle saw all his plans go awry…

In the previous year the Bishop of Glasgow, Robert Boyd, a protégé of Morton, had died. Glasgow lay within the district of the Lennox, therefore the Duke of Lennox, as hereditary Baillie of the bishopric, had the right to name his successor. Lennox put forward the minister of Stirling, a man named Robert Montgomerie, under terms that left the revenues of the see in his promoter's hands. Furthermore, in addition to an annual stipend of £1,000 Scots, Montgomerie was given both horse-corn and poultry. This was far more than was usually paid to ministers of the Kirk. 'A vile bargain it was' wrote Spottiswoode, who, later to become the Archbishop of St Andrews, was then a young man. Montgomerie, excommunicated by the Kirk, was reinstated by the King and Council on the grounds that the Kirk's punishment was illegal.

The unfortunate Bishop Montgomerie, however, castigated by the General Assembly when it met in the spring of 1582, had to be protected by an armed guard when he entered Glasgow, where riots broke out upon his arrival. Attempting to preach a sermon in the cathedral, he was hustled out of the building, the door locked behind him, while a minister preached on the text 'He that entereth not by the door but by the window is a thief and a robber.' Lennox rescued him, taking him to Dalkeith, while the ministers threatened to excommunicate the duke for his defiance, a threat which he entirely ignored. But his enemies, largely inspired by religion, began to conspire against him.

In the spring of 1582, the disgruntled nobles united themselves in a bond to get rid of the Catholic influences surrounding the young King. The historian David Calderwood, writing that they called themselves the 'Lords Enterprisers,' named them as the Earls of Mar and Gowrie, the Master of Glamis, the Laird of Easter-Wemyss, Lewis Bellenden, Lord Boyd, Lord Lindsay, the Abbots of Dunfermline, Dryburgh and Paisley, the Prior of Pittenweem and the Constable of Dundee. Not surprisingly amongst them was John Cunningham, the laird of Drumquhassle, now furiously resentful of both the favourites who had undermined his own influence over the King.

In July James went on a progress to Perth, Lennox as usual by his side. Hardly had they arrived there, however, before Andrew Melville, the Scottish theologian and religious reformer (uncle of Sir James Melville of Halhill) appeared at the head of a party of ministers bringing a list of 'Griefs' from the Kirk. First of these was that the King, influenced by evil counsellors, had taken over the Kirk's authority, which belonged only to God. Most fervently did they oppose the appointment of Robert Montgomerie as Bishop of Glasgow. Melville gave the list of 'Griefs' to James, whereupon a furious bilingual shouting match broke out between Lennox and Melville. Following this, when the King and Lennox sat through a public sermon, insults were hurled at Lennox to his face.

Furious, he leapt to his feet, yelling back obscenities, until the King jumped up and put his hand over his mouth while he and Peter Young (James's former tutor) hauled him back into his seat.

During the King's absence, Robert Montgomerie was unwise enough to appear in Edinburgh, carrying a royal proclamation of his authority. Raising his voice to shout above the crowd, he was met by a hail of stones and rotten eggs which sent him scurrying back to Dalkeith. James was so amused when told of it that he lay down on the Inch of Perth, rolling about in helpless laughter. Rising at last to his feet, he said the bishop was 'a seditious loon' and that he would no longer protect him. Lennox, however, saw the more serious side of the matter and persuaded the King that they should hold a Chamberlain Eyre, or Judicial Court, in Edinburgh so that the most dangerous ministers of the Kirk could be arrested and after trial imprisoned, 'for sedition and popular commotion.'[38]

Meanwhile, as Lennox went to Dalkeith Castle to construe the details of the forthcoming litigation, due to take place in Glasgow on 27 July, James gave himself a holiday and with only a few companions, went deer hunting at the invitation of the ever loyal, Roman Catholic, Earl of Atholl.

Aware of this and knowing that while Lennox was at Dalkeith, Arran was at his own house of Kinneil (to the west of Boness near Edinburgh) his enemies, motivated by their hatred of his favourites, prepared to act. Approaching Lord Gowrie they asked him to act as their leader. Gowrie (always it seems inclined to vacillation) was indecisive, unwilling to commit himself for fear of the inevitable forfeiture which would result if the attempt against the favourites failed. He was still undecided when the laird of Drumquhassle, told him that he had certain knowledge Lennox intended to kill him upon their first meeting. [39]

Drumquhassle, who in his hatred of Morton, had originally suggested to James that he should summon his cousin from France, had been much put out when the King had appointed Lennox Captain of Dumbarton Castle. This meant that, demoted to being his deputy, Drumquhassle lost the perquisites the post contained to Sir William Stewart of Caverston. Deeply offended, Drumquhassle had gone to Robert Bowes, the English Ambassador, for advice. Bowes, on Queen Elizabeth's direction, had then suggested that he held Dumbarton Castle against Lennox, refusing to relinquish his authority. Furiously resentful, he then aimed only at Lennox's destruction, turning over possibilities in his mind as to how that might be obtained.

His deer hunting over, James returned to Perth to be waylaid by Lord Gowrie who invited him to stay the night at his nearby castle of Ruthven, a short way beyond the city walls. James accepted joyfully, never thinking for a moment that he was walking into a trap. Thus, on the evening of 22 August, the King came to Ruthven Castle to find himself amongst fellow guests in the persons of the nobles calling themselves the Enterprisers. Still unsuspecting he woke up next morning, eager to ride on to Edinburgh, but as he opened the door of his bedroom, ready to make his way down the spiral stair to the hall, he found his way barred by several of the Lords Enterprisers. Frightened, he tried to push past them, but the Master of Glamis 'laid his leg across the door' and ordered the King to stay within.

James knew he was trapped. Shouting loud invectives, he then burst into tears as he heard Lord Gowrie saying, words so humiliating that they would haunt his mind for the rest of his life, 'It is no matter of his tears, better that bairns should weep than bearded men.' [40]

In November 1582 d'Aubigny wrote to King James, advising him most strongly not to accept the advice of the Earls of Gowrie and Mar and in particular the Laird of Drumquhassle, whom he believed to be at the heart of the clique of his enemies, intent on his destruction as the leader of the Catholic party in Scotland.

Nothing, however, could be proven against him and Drumquhassle was released to live, with his wife Janet, and their family of six sons and three daughters at his seat of Drumquhassle Castle near the Stirlingshire village of Drymen, while attending the Privy Council when summoned. [41]

Following the Raid of Ruthven, as it came to be called, the Lords Enterprisers held the King prisoner for ten months, moving him first to Edinburgh and then to Stirling, always under close guard. Arran tried to rescue him, boasting that he would chase all the lords into mouse holes, but was chased himself and took refuge in the house of Ruthven. Most of the Lords Enterprisers were all for making an end of him, but he was saved by Lord Gowrie's intervention, much, as Melville put it, 'to his own wreck afterwards.' The Duke of Lennox, told of this happening, was more circumspect, retiring into the safety of his own well-guarded Dumbarton Castle. From there, according to the same source, 'he passed through England to France, where he shortly died of a sickness contracted through displeasure.' [42]

Arran, meanwhile, remained Lord Gowrie's prisoner. It seemed that the lords had triumphed. The King was helpless in their hands.

But James had contrived to call a convention at St Andrews to which, by letters, presumably smuggled out, he summoned some of the nobility. They included the Earls of Huntly, Argyll, Montrose, Crawford, Rothes and March and surprisingly the Earl of Gowrie, now apparently bitterly aware that Cunningham of Drumquhassle's assertion that Lennox was plotting to murder him was untrue. Therefore, he repeatedly promised James to try in any way he could, to set him free from the Calvinistic Presbyterians who were holding him, in his own castles, a prisoner in everything but name.

Assured of the presence of the men he had summoned to the convention, the King sent a Colonel Stewart, now in the absence of Arran, Captain of the Guard, a man he knew he could trust, to Sir James Melville asking him for his advice on how to set himself free. Melville obeyed the summons most unwillingly, having retired from the court, determined to live a quiet life. Nonetheless, his conscience pricked by a sense of duty, he rode to join the King at Falkland where James lamented, 'his hard state and mishandling by his own subjects.' Melville advised him not to commit himself entirely to the opponents of the Ruthven Raiders, suggesting that, if only to avoid further discord, they should be pardoned. James then said that he was determined to free himself fully or to die in the attempt.

Acting, it would seem on Melville's advice, the King then accepted an invitation from the old bishop, his great uncle (who, after relinquishing the title of Earl of Lennox on James' request to d'Aubigny, had become the Earl of March and Lord Dunbar) to stay with him at St Andrews for a day or two before the convention of the council. Conveniently, he found an excuse for doing so in that March's, 'preparation of wild meat and other flesh fleshes, would spoil in case his Majesty came not to make good cheer with him some days before.'

Immediately there was a protest from those guarding the King, that some of their more powerful counterparts could not make it to St Andrews in time to prevent any attempts on his part to set himself free of their control. Nonetheless, ignoring them, James rode from Falkland to St Andrews, a distance of some thirty miles. Reaching there he lodged first in the old inns, where the yard dykes or walls at the ends of the gardens were the building's only defence. James was nevertheless delighted, feeling himself like a bird let out of its cage. Melville, who had joined the King at St Andrews, told him that he would be safer if he lodged in the castle for the Lords Enterprisers would realise that he had escaped and inevitably try to capture him again. James supped at the inn, for some reason, 'loth to enter within the castle.' But, acting on Melville's advice, he did sleep there and the next morning the lords, summoned by his secret letters, joined him there to his unimaginable delight.

The Lords Enterprisers, warned too late of what was happening, rode like furies for St Andrews but, on trying to enter the town, found themselves faced by heralds, carrying a proclamation forbidding them to approach the King and commanding them to, 'retire to their houses, till he should take further order.' Gowrie, alone, was allowed to come to the King before whom he fell on his knees, begging his forgiveness for restraining him in his own castle and in particular for offences against the Duke of Lennox and his own person. James, magnanimous in his triumph, granted him the pardon he requested.[43]

Heartbroken over the death of Lennox, in the autumn of 1583 James sent for his beloved cousin's eldest son, Ludovic Stuart, aged only nine, who, on 13 November, landed at Leith. Met by three earls, he was conducted to the King at Holyrood Palace. James received him with great happiness and immediately invested him with all the lands and honours he had given to his father during his time in Scotland.

It was through the winter months that followed that the King, still grieving for his beloved cousin, composed the poem called 'Ane Metaphoricall Invention of a Tragedy called Phoenix.' Throughout his childhood he had heard the story, told originally by the now dead herald, Sir David Lindsay of the Mount, when tutor to his father, James V, of how, when a little boy, his father had been given a pet parakeet. The bird, much prized by its owner and thought one of the wonders of the world by the court, had escaped into Stirling Park, where, pecked to death by carrion, it had met an untimely end. Now, in his sadness, the tale recurring to his mind, James realised the co-incidence of the two events, comparing Lennox to an exotic, Arabian bird, which had mysteriously flown into Scotland.

He described how he had tamed it, an obvious allusion to the religious conversion of Lennox, and how the Phoenix, loved and admired originally by all the smaller birds, had by night perched in his chamber. But then, inevitably, had come the jealousy, as birds of prey, plainly the Lords Enterprisers, had driven the beautiful Phoenix to its death.

Disarmingly, in a prelude to his poem, he decried his ability as a writer, 'But knowing myself so unskilful and grosse to translate any of his heavenly and learned works, I almost left it off and was ashamed of that opinion also.' But, nonetheless, he did continue to write the poem, his lament for the cousin he had loved.

'Then fra I saw (as I already told)
How men complaind for things whilk might amend,
How David Lindsay did complaine of old
His Papingo, her death, and sudden end,
Ane common foule, whose kinde be all is kend,
All these hes moved me presently to tell
Ane Tragedie, in griefs thir to excel…

In Arabie cald Foelix was she bred
This foule, excelling Iris farr in hew,
Whose body whole, with purpour was owercledd,
Whose tail of coulour was celestiall blew,
With skarlat pennis that through it mixed grew,
Her craig (head) was like the yallowe burnisht gold,
And she her self thre hundredth yeare was old…

In quantitie, she dois resemble neare
Unto the foule of mightie love, by name
The Aegle calld: oft in the time of yeare,
She usde to soir, and flie through diuers realme,
Out through the Azure skes, whill she did shame
The Sunne himself, her coulour was so bright,

Till he abashit beholding such a light.

He continues to describe how this mythical bird flew across Asia and then Europe to reach Scotland where 'The winter came, and storms cled all the fields' so that she flew into a house where he began to tame her. Then, the other birds, growing jealous, started to attack her. She fled to him for protection:

'For then they made her as a common prey
To them, of whome she looked for no deare,
They strake at her so bitterly, whill feare.
Stayde other fowlis to preis for to defend her
From thir ingrate, whilks now had clene miskend her.'

She flew away, back to where she was bred, 'where storms dois neuer blow' but James sent a messenger to find her. He returned with tragic news.

'And syne he tolde, how she had such desyre
To burne her self, as she sat downe therein.
Syne how the Sunne the withered stra did fyre,
Which brunt her nest, her fethers, bones and skin
All turnd in ash...'

But inevitably, as the sun disappears to rise again, the Phoenix rose from the ashes, James, perhaps alluding to Lennox's son, young Ludovic, just arrived in Scotland, wrote:

'Draw farr from heir, mount heigh up through the air,
To gar thy heat and beames be law and near.
That in this countrey, which is colde and bair.
Thy glistring beames als ardent may appeir
As they were oft in Arabie: so heir
Let them be now, to mak ane Phoenix new
Euen of this worme of Phoenix ashe which grew.

CHAPTER 13

The Return of Arran
'Throat Cutters to Assist Him'

The departure and death of Lennox left a void of power in Scotland. James, still only seventeen, needed a strong man behind him. He found one in his other former favourite, James Stewart, whom he had created Earl of Arran. Sir James Melville and Colonel Stewart, now Captain of the Palace Guard, formerly friends of Lennox, did all they could to dissuade the King from reinstating Arran, but the King refused to listen and in August summoned Arran to court.

Arran, from all accounts, was a man of charismatic character. Described as possessing 'a magnificent presence' he quite literally dazzled the seventeen-year-old King. Soon he became predominant to the point where, having proved himself a good administrator, James consulted him on every matter. So strong was his influence, that only a year after his return to favour, he advised the young King to proclaim himself the head, not only of the government, but of the Kirk. As such James ruled that the church should be controlled by bishops and that he and the Council should have power over all people clerical and lay. Church assemblies could be held only with his personal permission, while public utterances against either himself or the Council, would result in penalties and prison.

The next to succumb to the might of the King's new power, was William Ruthven, the Earl of Gowrie, he who had invited the King to stay with him at Ruthven Castle on that ill-fated night when he was returning from his hunting expedition in Atholl. Melville graphically described how:

'Those of the nobility who were now in fear of their estates fled, others were banished. He (Arran) shot directly at the life and lands of the Earl of Gowrie, for the Highland oracles had shown unto his wife that Guthrie would be ruined, as she told to some of her familiars. But she helped that prophesy forward as well as she could: for Gowrie had been his first master, and despised his insolent pride, and misbehaviour plainly in council, which few others durst do, therefore he hated his person, and loved his lands, which length he obtained.'[44]

In April 1583 the erstwhile supporters of Lord Gowrie, desperate for English support, sent an embassy to London. They asked that, in return for a close alliance, Elizabeth should grant the English estates of his grandfather, the murdered Earl of Lennox, to King James to whom, in view of his great need for money, she should also send a gift of £10,000 to be followed by an annual pension of £500.

It was the English ambassador Sir Robert Bowes, who reported back to Queen Elizabeth, in the August of 1583, that a plot was on hand to punish the Laird of Drumquhassle for making alleged treachery against both the King and the government, which included surrendering Dumbarton Castle to the English. Drumquhassle was ordered by the King and the Privy Council to imprisonment in Blackness Castle, one of Scotland's strongest defences on the Forth, a command, which with little alternative and promised that his life would be spared, he obeyed.

Within the walls of his prison Drumquhassle, now in his late fifties and with the cold of the prison no doubt worsening the pain in arthritic bones, may yet have felt himself fortunate to be at least alive. Nonetheless, in the hours of enforced idleness, which prisoners were forced to endure, his mind must have seethed with bitterness for the cruelty of his fate. Fortune which had favoured him to rise, albeit thanks partly to nepotism, from the obscurity of a mere country laird to be Master of the King's Household in Stirling Castle and governor of Dumbarton Castle, that great protector of the Lennox, the area of which, as the Earl's factor, he had virtually held control, now seemed to have kicked him in the teeth. Why, he must have asked himself, had he not foreseen how the renowned charm and person of d'Aubigny, whom, so inadvertently, he himself had suggested should be brought to Scotland, would captivate the King's mind? Undoubtedly, when the news reached Scotland of d'Aubigny's untimely death in France, Drumquhassle must have rejoiced in

89

hearing that the man, who had repaid him for the great favour he had done him, by turning the King's mind against him, had died so quickly upon his return to his native land. Obsessed with hatred, during the months of idleness, he carefully planned his revenge.

Queen Elizabeth, in the meanwhile, had plans of her own. Assuming that James had still some sense of duty, if not of actual affection for the mother he could not remember, she envisaged a Scottish alliance in which, Mary might be released from captivity, provided that both her son and the King of France would guarantee her compliance with Elizabeth's terms. But James thought otherwise. To the English Queen's ambassador Robert Bowes, he explained that he had discovered that his mother, if released, intended to return to Scotland as the Queen regnant, to take precedence over himself. He had told her these terms were unacceptable. Her involvement with Catholic powers in Europe made her unfit to rule Scotland, or for that matter England, should she, in the event of Elizabeth's death, inherit her cousin's throne. Told this, Elizabeth's negotiations with Mary ended and the reason for bribing James with money to extract him from his mother's influence, disappeared.

James had in fact been in contact both with the Duke of Guise in France and with Philip II of Spain. Both he and Arran are believed to have been contemplating an invasion of England to gain the support of these Catholic monarchs when there arrived in Scotland the Master of Gray.

Patrick Master of Gray, the eldest son of Lord Gray, had been one of Queen Mary's agents in France. He returned to Scotland with Ludovic, the son of d'Aubigny, now, since his father's death, the second Duke of Lennox. Melville says rather mysteriously, that Gray was in the King's confidence and that through some of her friends in France, he was conveying letters to and fro Queen Mary, his imprisoned mother in England. He was also carrying out a secret liaison between the Queen and some of the English Catholics. Certainly, on a previous mission, when sent to Portugal by Queen Elizabeth to congratulate King Henry I on his succession, Gray, on his return journey, had been granted an audience with King Philip II of Spain and thus knew him to be much averse to supporting an invasion of England on behalf of the Scottish King.

Realising now that Queen Mary's cause was hopeless and that furthermore, neither Guise nor King Philip, was ready to come to her aid, he was ready to change his allegiance. It was absolutely essential, so he made clear to James, that he must cultivate a friendship with Queen Elizabeth as his best hope of achieving his over-riding ambition of eventually succeeding to her throne.

This was the reason why, in August 1584, the King sent the Master of Gray to London to represent him in the negotiations, still continuing between his mother and Queen Elizabeth, as to the former's possible release. It was only when, after the ambassador's return to Scotland, that Queen Mary received a letter from her son informing her, that he could not be involved in a treaty with her while she remained Elizabeth's prisoner.

Believing he had betrayed her, Mary raged in fury, calling down curses on his head while James, for his part, denied that he had ever promised to form an association with Queen Elizabeth by which she might be freed. It was the end of all contact. He never wrote to her again.

Then came news that the Earl of Gowrie, hanging about in Dundee, as Melville said 'by nature over slow' had been taken prisoner and executed. Gowrie had in fact been on the point of leaving the country, but as he was waiting for his ship to be ready in Dundee, he was told that the Earls of Mar and Angus and the Master of Glamis, who had fled to Ireland, were plotting to come back to Scotland and seize the town and castle of Stirling from where they would raise an army to overthrow Arran. Greatly excited, Gowrie decided to join them. But the King got wind of his loitering in Dundee and then had a dream in which he saw the Earl of Gowrie taken prisoner and brought before him by Colonel Stewart, Captain of the Guard. James wished to spare him, but Arran, intent on getting his land, persuaded others to give evidence against him so that, with a so-called charge of treachery proved against him, the King had no alternative other than to order him to be hanged. The sentence was carried out on 28 May 1584.

Gowrie died bravely, declaring that he had been no more an enemy of Lennox than the rest of the Lords Enterprisers. He prayed that his blood would not be on the head of the King. Most emphatically, he proved himself a devout Christian so that many who watched his execution felt that he had been gravely wronged.

According to both the religious historians, Bishop Spottiswoode and Calderwood 'On the Earl of Gowrie's apprehension, the Earls of Angus and Mar, with others, fled to England' and in order to breed a terror in the people and cause them abstain from communicating in any sort with the exiled Lords, a proclamation was made that, 'whosoever should discover any person offending in that kind should, besides his own pardon, receive a special reward.'[45]

CHAPTER 14
The Doomed Conspiracy

The bribe thus offered was too much for one man to resist. 'Hereupon did one Robert Hamilton of Eglismachen, delate Malcolm Douglas of Mains and John Cunningham of Drumquhassle, for having conspired to intercept the King in hunting, and detain him in some stronghold till the Lords might come and receive him' …

To make out the accusation, it was devised that Sir James Edmonstone of Duntreath, who had lived in great familiarity with both Hamilton and Cunningham, should be charged with the same crime, and upon his confession be pardoned, which, by the policy of the accuser, to his own personal discredit, he was menaced to yield unto. [46]

In plainer words what had happened was that John Cunningham, the Laird of Drumquhassle, arch schemer that he was, brooding on his hatred of the King's favourites, who had suborned him, had contrived to remain in touch with the exiled lords. Intent on a chance of revenge and at the same time of re-instating himself in the King's favour, he had formed a plan to return them to Scotland. To do so he had roped in two of his neighbours, both men of the Lennox, and local lairds. One was his son-in-law, Malcolm Douglas of Mains, the other James Edmonstone of Duntreath, whose land, adjacent to Drumquhassle's, lay in the Blane Valley some twelve miles north of Glasgow.

Duntreath Castle, built round a courtyard into which cattle were driven for safety when Highlanders raided from the north, was a place of defence. To there, in the darkness of a December night, came a man on horseback. Heavily cloaked to avoid both recognition and the cold, Black John Hume of the Law, on two separate occasions, brought letters of credit from his patron, the exiled Earl of Mar.

The Laird of Duntreath, then in his early forties, was a man of some standing. In 1578 he had obtained from Colin Earl of Argyll, the Justice-General of Scotland, the grant of a deputation for holding justiciary courts at the fortalice of Duntreath, upon the criminals therein named. Then, six years later, he had received the 'escheat' of Mungo Edmonstone, brother of James of Newton, the captain of Doune Castle, for the former's treachery at the late 'suprizal of the Castle of Sterling.' Following this, when the Earl of Gowrie was brought before Mr James Graham sitting as Justice, Sir James Edmonstone was present as his co-juror.

The King, knowing that there was strong feeling against his favourites, made a public proclamation that anyone informing against agitators would receive, not only a pardon, but a special reward.

Sir James would seem to have been in debt. The family history shows that he had done much building at Duntreath Castle. Also five daughters needed dowries when they married. He later admitted that 'he had been led to make a confession of a threefold conspiracy of the exiled lords against the King, of which he had been informed by Black John Hume of the Law, who came twice to him, each time with a letter of credit from the Earl of Mar, the knowledge of which now preyed upon his conscience.'[47]

But through his family connections he was, in the words of a contemporary, 'the Duke of Lennox's man' and as such, as a Lennox vassal, held his land from the King.

Subsequently, Edmonstone met and connived with Drumquhassle in the kirks of both Blanefield and Killearn, then described as 'mean buildings,' probably constructed of rough stone roofed with turf or thatch, not comparable with the nineteenth century churches of today.

There, in the close, dark interiors, thinking themselves safe from eavesdroppers, they made three separate plans. The first was that a force of a thousand or twelve hundred men would be raised, to surround Holyrood House and take the King prisoner. The second, that owing to the difficulty of procuring such a number, thirty or forty able men would be hired 'to await upon his Majesty in the fields, when his horse was souped (tired) and to carry him off, either to the house of Douglas (of Mains), or to Cumleye (Cumbrae?), or to an island in Loch Lomond. The third plot, was that since so many men could not be collected as even thirty or forty, without being suspected, every one of the principal conspirators, the Abbot of Aberbrothick, the Earls of Angus and Mar and the Master of Glamis, should each select two or three of their own men, who should secretly repair to wherever the King was residing, and having disguised themselves, and with their horses, tails, manes, and ears cut off, should pass over and kill the King, by shot or other weapon.'

'A ridiculous tale' as Hume of Godscroft justly calls it, but nevertheless, full in accordance with the spirit of the times.[48]

Someone must have talked too much. Somehow the conspiracy was discovered. Colonel Stewart was sent to arrest Mains and Drumquhassle, who, found in their own homes, surrendered without resistance. Stewart then took them as prisoners to Edinburgh, where, on 9 February 1585, they were presented before the Justice Mr John Graham.

As cunningly planned by Robert Hamilton of Eglismachan, the trial was a pre-arranged farce. The laird of Duntreath, who, apparently under threat of torture, had agreed to act as his dupe, was the first to be indicted, accused by Hamilton, together with his two neighbours, Douglas of Mains and Cunningham of Drumquhassle, for conspiracy to take and detain the King, in the manner aforesaid. All three were convicted, declared guilty of treason but doom was pronounced only upon Drumquhassle and Mains, both of whom, on the same day, were hanged in the public street of Edinburgh. Duntreath, as promised by Hamilton, was spared.

So died John Cunningham, the laird of Drumquhassle, a man who through exploitation of his relations, had achieved both the power and the prominence of his greatest ambition. Self-seeking, as Melville described him, this most duplicitous of conspirators, had finally over-played his hand. Some even lamented him, largely because at the age of nearly seventy, he was now old by the standards of the time. But it was Douglas of Mains whose end was thought unjustified, he being a much respected man.

It was the Earl of Arran, one of a kind with Drumquhassle, who believing himself secure in the favour of Queen Elizabeth, had suggested to James that he should send the young man over whom he believed he had control, the handsome Master of Gray to England. Gray had departed, in October 1584, with instructions to arrange an Anglo-Scottish alliance. He had succeeded in doing so to the point where, in the following year, Elizabeth had sent Sir Edward Wotton to Scotland with a present of horses, to the huge delight of the Scottish King, together with an offer of £4,000 down and the same amount yearly thereafter to guarantee the promulgation of a league made in July 1585.[49]

James was so pleased that he said he would agree to any terms that the English Queen offered without even consulting his Council. 'The King is so eager in the matter of the amity' reported Wotton, 'that I fear nothing, if her Majesty is pleased to take hold of it, as is hoped here.'[50]

All seemed settled, but then suddenly came disaster, bad enough to upset any treaty with England, when Sir Francis Russell, son of the Earl of Bedford, was killed in a fight on the Borders by one of Arran's men. The King, paralysed with misery, wept like a child, refusing to either eat or drink for twenty-four hours. Arran was imprisoned in the castle of St Andrews, from where, Wotton, in a most unchristian spirit, hoped, most fervently, that he might be sent to England to be hanged.

Yet within a few days Arran was forgiven, to reappear, arrogant as ever, in his own house of Kinneil near Edinburgh. Queen Elizabeth, told of this happening, promptly decided to precipitate trouble in Scotland by allowing the refugee Protestant lords of the Gowrie faction to return.

In October 1885 the outlawed lords, Angus, Mar and the Master of Glamis, 'licensed' by Queen Elizabeth, crossed the border from England into their own land to return to Scotland. Reaching Berwick they were joined by the Hamiltons and their allies, who included Francis, now the 5th Earl of Bothwell, a handsome, fair-haired young man. With them also was Captain James Cunningham, a younger brother of the late Drumquhassle.[51]

The combined army marched by way of Kelso and Falkirk to lay siege to Stirling Castle on 2 November, where Arran, knowing the King to be within the castle, hastened to join him. Fulminating against Gray, he poured libellous accusations against him into James's ear, threatening to murder him as a traitor.

But at sight of the Protestant lord's army gathering beneath the walls, Arran fled. Terrified James tried to follow him through a postern gate, but only to find it securely locked by Gray, who then successfully contrived to convince the King of his first minister's connivance against the proposed agreement with England.

Arran, the second son of Lord Ochiltree, a man of no great inheritance, who by his own duplicity and force of character had contrived to become Lord Chancellor of Scotland through his domination of the King, now knew his power to be gone. Through his double dealings with the Master of Gray, the man he himself had had urged James to send to England to treat with Queen Elizabeth, he had fallen into disgrace. Desperate to avoid the humiliation of a trial, which could too easily lead to execution, he retired to live in obscurity in Ayrshire.

But his enemies did not forget him. The Douglasses had long memories, steadfastly plotting vengeance. Ten years were to pass before, on 5 December 1595, Arran was murdered by Sir James Douglas of Parkhead, nephew of the Regent Morton, the man over whose own execution he had so triumphantly rejoiced.

Arran had many enemies, none of them more vehement in their hatred than Sir James Melville. After a vicious quarrel he wrote:

'I would get more honest men to take my part than he would get throat-cutters to assist him.' Then on another occasion, after a further altercation, 'He made the whole subjects to tremble under him, and every man depended upon him, daily inventing and seeking out new faults against divers, to get the gift of their escheats, lands, benefices, and to procure bribes. He vexed the whole writers and lawyers to make sure his gifts and acquisitions. Those of the nobility who were now in fear of their estates, fled; others were banished.'[52]

Amongst them was the inquisitor, Hamilton of Eglismachen, who, living in constant fear, having taken refuge in Stirling Castle, clinging to Arran's power, on the latter's escape made his own desperate attempt to gain freedom. Then, according to Calderwood, James Johnston of Wardraw, pretending he had made a vow to avenge Douglas of Mains's death, 'did kill him

97

as he was flying through the park, on the south side of (Stirling) town.' Likewise, the laird of Duntreath, constantly in fear of reprisal, eventually accepted the King's offer to become a 'settler' in Northern Ireland. [53]

CHAPTER 15
The Price of a Mother's Life

Following the lord's raid on Stirling Queen Elizabeth wrote to James expressing her astonishment that the men to whom she had granted permission to go to Germany, ended up so strangely in Scotland. James replied that he wished to deal as honestly with the Queen of England as she had done with him and gave her his sworn word that never had he dealt with any foreign country against her. Pacified, she then agreed to renewed negotiations for a league of mutual support as had been already suggested.

In March 1586 she sent Thomas Randolph to Edinburgh to ask the King to sign articles providing for the defence of the true religion and for mutual assistance in the case of attack from abroad. James, all too willing to agree, asked only for a pension of £5,000 (which the frugal Queen reduced to £4,000) and formal recognition of his right, on her death, to succeed her as England's king.

The treaty once formally signed, on 2 July 1586, Elizabeth expressed her goodwill with a present of fallow deer. Met by the King at Musselburgh, the animals were then ferried across the Forth to Falkland to be 'entertained honourably with bran, oats and hay in a fair park to shift for themselves' as Randolph, with much amusement wrote.[54]

Meanwhile, in England Queen Mary's involvement in the schemes of a young man called Anthony Babington, to assassinate Queen Elizabeth and then with Spanish help put Mary on the throne of England as a Catholic queen, was discovered by Sir Francis Walsingham. Arrested on 3 August, the Queen had her papers seized and her servants interrogated.

James did not think then that her life was in danger, believing that she would just be more closely guarded. Questioned by Walsingham, he said that although he could not agree to her execution, he cared not how closely she was imprisoned. 'Let her be put in the Tower or some other firm manse and kept from intelligence' he suggested.

But in September, he received an alarming letter from Archibald Douglas, the lawyer employed to act on his behalf in London, warning him that his mother was now likely to be killed. Douglas advised him not to interfere on her behalf because Elizabeth, if enraged, might put an end to his succession. Thus he must choose between trying to save his mother's life, and his hopes of the English throne.

Under great pressure in Scotland, James told Douglas to do everything possible to save his mother, telling him to 'deal very earnestly with the Queen and her councillors for our sovereign mother's life,' but at the same time, making sure that 'our title to that Crown be not prejudiced.' This was followed by another letter in which he told Douglas that he was sending 'an honourable embassy' to Elizabeth who, 'if she could see his heart would discover a jewel of honest meaning locked in a coffer of perplexity. Guess ye in what strait my honour will be in, this disaster being perfected, since before God I dare scarce, for crying out of the whole people go abroad...so is the whole of Scotland incensed with this matter.'

When Elizabeth saw this letter, which Douglas disloyally showed her, she flew into a rage, believing that, to save his mother, James would break the treaty signed only three months before. On the same day Douglas met the Earl of Leicester to confer with him secretly in his carriage. Leicester said openly that Mary's death would prove much to her son's benefit and then asked him openly, what Elizabeth most wanted to know, if James would break the league with England if such a thing took place. Douglas replied that, in his opinion, it would not.

On 14 December, as news of this conversation reached him, James faced a heart breaking quandary as he realised that the only way to save his mother's life was to sever the treaty with England of such vital importance to himself.

Convulsed with indecision, he wrote two letters, one to Elizabeth, telling her he was sending an embassy to London, the other to Leicester assuring him that he had not been corresponding with his mother. To Queen Elizabeth he declared that his mother's death would be a sad return for the friendship he had shown her. He begged her to be compassionate and to let her be sent to France under guarantee of her promise to refrain from future conspiracies. When the Master of Gray, one of the ambassadors, suggested that Queen Mary, if pardoned, should make over her claims to the throne of Scotland to her son, Elizabeth told him sharply to tell his King what good she had done for him in holding his crown over his head since he was born, and that, "I mind to keep the league that now stands between us, and if he breaks it, it shall be a double fault."

The embassy a failure, James wrote the English queen a final letter. If Elizabeth knew of his difficulties in Scotland and of all the universal hatred of his mother's death would have on other rulers, she would have mercy on him. Elizabeth was unmoved. In her last prison of Fotheringhay Castle, in Northamptonshire, Mary was beheaded on 9 February 1587.

CHAPTER 16
The Fragile Reins of Power

In May 1587, three months after his mother's death, King James celebrated his majority by holding a Parliament in Edinburgh. Summoned by royal proclamation the lords of the realm attended to be entertained in Holyrood Palace by what was described as a love-feast. James begged his subjects to forgo the long established feuds which had bedevilled the peace of the country for so many generations past. Solemnly, following the banquet, men whose ancestors had fought with each other for centuries, walked hand in hand from Holyrood up to the Mercat Cross. There the King drank to them while they toasted each other, their voices drowned by a deafening cannonade fired from the ramparts of the castle. The people, gathered to watch the spectacle, hallooed with happiness but amongst them few, if any, believed that that this so-called show of goodwill was anything other than a charade.

James at the age of twenty, was a slim young man with broad shoulders who, thanks to the deformity of his right foot, walked with a distinctive unbalanced stride. Regarded by most of his peers as a puppet ruler of what amounted to a collection of federal states, he found himself confronted by his most powerful subjects, men like the young Earl of Argyll, omnipotent in the north-west, and Huntly, colossus of the north-east.

The power of such nobles lay in the number of men they could call to arms. Thanks to the now dominant strength of the Campbell Earls of Argyll and Calder the MacDonalds, the once Lords of the Isles, were a spent force. The last Lord had died a hundred years before, and Angus MacDonald of Islay, acknowledged chief of Clan Donald, was now living in the glens of Antrim. Elsewhere, throughout Scotland, the Highland chiefs and the Lowland lords, forever keen to take umbrage, clung tenaciously to their power.

James was shrewd enough to realise that the only possible way to subdue the violence that so ruined the stability of his country, was stronger enforcement of the law. To this aim he turned for advice to Sir John Maitland, the man who, originally his Secretary, had just become Chancellor of the realm. John Maitland of Thirlestane was a brother of William Maitland of Lethington, the great protagonist of Queen Mary, who had died apparently by his own hand following the collapse of her party after the capture of Edinburgh Castle. Described by Bishop Spottiswoode, as 'a man of rare parts, of deep wit and full of courage and most faithful to his King and master,' the prelate added of John Maitland that 'no man ever carried himself in his place more wisely nor sustained it more courageously against his enemies than he did.'

Moreover, in addition to these qualities, he had many others that particularly endeared him to James. Writing both English and Latin verse he was possessed of a sharp Scots tongue. He loved both raillery and sarcasm, and mingled great matters of state with jests and facetiousness, to the great amusement of his sovereign. [55]

John Maitland had entered the King's service through the auspices of Esmé Stuart, he who had been made Duke of Lennox by his devoted cousin King James. But Maitland – described by the Earl of Bothwell as a mere paddock-stool (toadstool) - was not of aristocratic birth. Inevitably, for this reason, his dominance and the reforms he suggested, namely; to improve the royal finances, to make closer contact with the Kirk and to provide for the defence of the realm by subduing the violence in the Borders, Highlands and Western Isles,[56] were regarded by the nobles as an infringement of their hereditary rights.

Maitland had many enemies, both Protestant and Catholic, most powerful amongst them the young Catholic Earls of Huntly, Errol and Angus together with the older Crawford. The King, while loyal to Maitland, nonetheless knew that he had to keep contact with the Catholic earls as a counterbalance to the power of the Kirk. Moreover he loved Huntly, who married to Lady Henrietta Stuart, a sister of Ludovic, the young Duke of Lennox, was one of his closest friends.

In Scotland, following the Queen's death, fury exploded against the English. In the parliament of July 1587, the Chancellor Sir John Maitland, made an impassioned speech demanding that her death be avenged, while the nobles, on their knees, swore to assist the King in doing so. To appease them he wrote to Henry III of France, to his mother and Mary's former mother-in-law Catherine de Medici, and to the Duke de Guise asking them for assistance in punishing those responsible for his mother's death.

Meanwhile at home James faced immediate danger from the Scottish nobility of the north where the Earls of Huntly, Crawford and Montrose, in cohesion with Lord Maxwell and Lord Claud Hamilton in the south, plotted to bring a Spanish army to Scotland. Threatened by the guns and re-enforced garrison of Edinburgh Castle, however, their attempt to raise a revolution in Dunfermline and Linlithgow failed.

The Catholic lords escaped retribution. James believed that they would fight for him in the event of the now expected Spanish invasion. Huntly, then seeking forgiveness, asked the King to a banquet at Dunfermline, but James, suspecting death by either a dagger or poison, riding a fast horse, in the first light of dawn fled the town to take refuge in Maitland's house in Edinburgh.

Once again he had escaped. No one, it seemed, could destroy the charmed life of this man, saved from before his birth by a pistol's misfire, target of would-be assassins over more than two decades, afraid yet defiant of destruction, when now in his twenty-second year.

In August 1588 a fleet of 130 Spanish warships, commanded by the Spanish Duke of Medina Sidonia, escorting an army to invade England, sailed from the port of Corunna. Warned of their coming, James offered Queen Elizabeth 'his forces, his person, and all that he commanded against yon strangers.' Yet none of this proved to be necessary, when, as is so well known, a great storm sent most of the ships to their doom. James, declaring the victory over the Spaniards to be 'far greater than that of David over the Philistines,' in a sonnet joyfully declared, that 'the nations had banded against the Lord, who had hurled them to destruction beneath the waves.'[57]

CHAPTER 17
Of Warlocks and Witches

King James was not to know that the next threat to destroy him would come, not from any earthly danger, but in a supernatural form. Likewise, little could he guess that his nemesis would prove to be a cousin, one of his own blood.

James Hepburn, the 4th Earl of Bothwell, third husband of Mary Queen of Scots, had been forfeited of all his titles and estates in 1567, when he fled from the battlefield of Carbery Hill. His nephew Francis, was the son of his sister, Jane Hepburn, Lady Morham, Mistress of Caithness, who had married John Stewart, the Prior of Coldingham, the illegitimate son of James V by his mistress Elizabeth Carmichael, being thus the first cousin of James VI.

Francis is believed to have been born in 1562 in his mother's house at Morham. At one time belonging to the Knights Templar, but for long part of the Bothwell estates, the village of Morham, hardly more than a hamlet, lay midway between Haddington and Gifford in what is now East Lothian, at the foot of the Lammermuir Hills.

Sometime during the 1530s, Patrick, 3rd Earl of Bothwell, had married Agnes Sinclair whom he had divorced within a decade. As part of her settlement he had given her the lands of Morham, after which she was styled as Dame Agnes Sinclair, Countess of Bothwell and Lady Morham. More commonly she was known simply as Lady Morham, living as she did in the Tower house of Morham until her death in 1572. The foundations of the small castle lie opposite the church, while the adjacent village has now disappeared.

Following the forfeiture of the 4th Earl of Bothwell, son of Dame Agnes, the land had fallen to the Crown. The superiority had then been granted to Sir Walter Scott of Buccleuch, but the Hepburns continued to hold the land by feu charter.

Francis Bothwell, while apparently spending his early years at Morham, the place where he was born, had been two years old when, in 1564, he was made Lord Badenoch and Enzie. A year later, when he was still only three, his aunt, Mary Queen of Scots, had given him a set of red serge bed curtains. In 1566, he had been made Commendator of Culross Abbey before, shortly afterwards becoming the lay holder of the rich benefices of Kelso Abbey in Roxburghshire, which, for some reason he then exchanged with the Chancellor, John Maitland of Thirlestane for Coldingham Priory.

On 10 January 1568, Francis, described as the Commendator of Coldingham, was granted a charter under the Great Seal of the lands and baronies formerly held by the Earls of Bothwell. These included large areas within the sheriffdoms of Edinburgh, Roxburgh, Lanark, Dumfries and Berwick and the Stewartries of Annandale and Kirkcudbright.[58]

On 27 November 1577, in the Great Hall of Stirling Castle, Francis was belted Earl of Bothwell by his cousin James VI. Four days later, at the age of fifteen, he was married to Margaret Douglas, daughter of the 7th Earl of Angus, widow of his suzerain, Sir Walter Scott, the laird of Buccleuch, in the Abbey of Holyrood House. The ceremony once over, he was ordered not to go within twenty miles of her 'for reassone of his youngnes.' Eventually, however, they were to have a large family believed to have consisted of no less than four sons and four daughters.

Thanks to his income from the monastic houses, after having first studied at St Andrews University, Francis had been able to go to the universities of both Paris and Rouen, before being recalled to Scotland by the King. He landed at Newhaven in June 1582.

On 29 May 1583, contrary to the advice of the 1st Lord Gowrie, who, with his confederates had controlled the King's movements since taking him prisoner in the 'Ruthven Raid' of the previous August of 1582, James left Edinburgh for Linlithgow. With him went the Earls of Mar, Angus, Bothwell and Marischal with whom he then proceeded to Falkland Palace.

Proof of Bothwell then being in the King's confidence emerges when, on 13 May 1585, he was amongst the lords commissioned to enforce the Warden of the Scottish Marches in dealing with the Border rebels. Then, more importantly, in June 1586, Bothwell was one of three commissioners whom James appointed to finalise a military alliance pact between the English and Scottish crowns, which was formally signed on 5 July.

Trouble began in the following year of 1587, when Bothwell was amongst the Scottish nobles who demanded that the death of the King's mother, Mary Queen of Scots, should be avenged by an invasion of England. King James, determined to somehow keep the peace with Queen Elizabeth, ordered Bothwell and his more vociferous protestors to be warded in Edinburgh Castle.

It would seem that while he was there, both he and the other lords involved in the raid on Stirling Castle in November 1585, took the chance to profess their innocence, blaming others over what had taken place. The King, perhaps with his tongue in his cheek, accepted their oaths and declared them to be his 'honest true servants.'

Following this, on 8 July 1587, Bothwell, as Keeper of Liddesdale, swore an obligation to the council to keep the peace in that area and on 29 July was made a full member of the Privy Council of Scotland of which he had already been an auxiliary member for at least five years.

Already Lord High Admiral of Scotland, an honour he had received with his earldom due to his close relationship with the King, he was ordered by James again to improve relations with Queen Elizabeth, to be ready to repel the Spanish Armada. On the strength of this, Bothwell took the chance to seize a Swedish ship, *Unicorn,* as a prize. But the council, when petitioned by its master, a man named Frederick Freis, ordered the Earl to return it to him within the space of twenty-four hours.

The King was at this time preoccupied with finding himself a wife. Ambassadors in the form of Peter Young, James's former tutor and now his Master Almoner and Colonel Stewart, Captain of the Palace Guard, had returned from Denmark, well satisfied with what they had found there. In particular, they had been much impressed by the fair young princesses and also by their father's reaction to the suggestion that the King of Scotland should send another embassy to Denmark in the following summer. King James put forward the name of Sir James Melville, but he, on the excuse of advancing age, declined. Subsequently, the chancellor, John Maitland of Thirlestane, sent off Peter Young again, together with the laird of Barnbarroch, the two of them being instructed to ask for marriage, in this case to the King of Denmark's eldest daughter, while at the same time sounding out King James's alleged rights to the Isles of Orkney, promised to Scotland as part of the dowry of that former Danish Princess who had married his great-great-grandfather James III.

Hardly had the ambassadors sailed then, however, than who should appear but Monsieur Dubartas, a French humanist and writer of divine poetry, who came as an envoy of the King of Navarre to offer the hand of that sovereign's sister to King James. The King liked Dubartas so much that it seemed that he would have postponed the ambassador's visit to Denmark had they not already embarked. Most emphatically, the chancellor Maitland of Thirlestane, assured the French envoy that the proposed marriage with a Danish princess would not now take place.

His reasons for doing so seem hard, if not almost impossible to understand. Suffice it to say that he made an implacable enemy of the new Queen of Scotland before she ever reached these shores.

As it was the King sent Sir James Melville's brother, Sir William Melville of Tongland to Denmark, who returned, not only with the portrait of the eldest princess, but praising her rare qualities. This proved all the more frustrating, as her father, it is thought at the instigation of the Queen of England, then married her off to the Duke of Brunswick. It was only thanks to the persistence of Colonel Stewart, who returned several times to Denmark at his own expense, that the King of Denmark, Frederic II, promised to give his second daughter, Princess Anne, as a bride to the Scottish king. Having done so, King Frederick II promptly died, but not before leaving instructions with his council and those made regents of the realm.

King James, understandably confused, decided to put the whole question of his marriage in the hands of God. Having prayed consistently for a fortnight, he then called his council together to tell them that he was resolved to marry in Denmark.

The decision, once made, he again asked Sir James Melville to go to Denmark as his ambassador to which, eventually, Melville reluctantly agreed. But time went on. No ship was prepared to sail, nor other preparations made. The council prevaricated, telling the King to ask advice of the Queen of England, while knowing full well that that she and her council would try to dissuade him from any marriage, just as she had done to his mother. Encouraged by Elizabeth's answer—she had even gone so far as to ask the King of Navarre to hold back the marriage of his sister for three years—the Scottish Council convened and, encouraged by Maitland, voted against the Danish marriage.

James retaliated with fury, disgusted at this untoward interference in his personal life. Inciting some of his servants to mutiny against the council and the chancellor, he threatened to kill the latter should he put any further stops on the marriage on which he had now set his mind. He announced that the Earl Marischal would be sent immediately to Denmark, taking with him his brother and the Constable of Dundee. But George Keith, the Earl Marischal, lacked credence to the point where he had to ask for sufficient power to conclude the treaty that the Danish King was being asked to sign. Desperately he sent back word to Lord Dingwall, who, fortunately found the King at Aberdeen, where, in the absence of the chancellor and most of the council, the contract and marriage ceremony was verified so that Anne was married, by proxy, in Copenhagen on 20 August 1589.

The new Queen of Scotland then set off with the Earl Marischal and an escort of her own people to sail to her husband's country. But terrible, unseasonal storms drove them onto the coast of Norway where they stayed until the weather improved.

The storm said to have been raised by the witches of Denmark, was admitted by some of them when they were burnt. The admiral of Denmark had given a cuff or a blow to one of the bailies of Copenhagen, whose wife, a witch herself, consulting with her associates in that art, raised the tempest to be revenged upon the said admiral. Devils crawled up the keel of the Queen's ship, or so it was claimed.

Meanwhile, in Scotland, King James waited impatiently for news of his coming bride. Needless to say he blamed Maitland, the chancellor, and the members of his council, who had so blatantly delayed the despatch of the ambassadors until the season of sailing was past. At a time when meteorology was still largely a mystery, storms howled throughout much of Western Europe causing a ferry to collide with a boat on the Firth of Forth, between Burntisland and Leith. Aboard the ferry was a lady called Jean Kennedy, who, married to James Melville's brother Sir Andrew Melville of Garvock, Master of the Household of Mary Queen of Scots during part of her imprisonment, had long been in England in attendance on the King's mother. Her son, King James, for this reason, trusting her integrity, had specially chosen Jean Kennedy to be a lady-in-waiting to his queen. Nothing would stop her boarding the ferry, which sank when it drifted into the boat. All but two on board were drowned, a crime to which the witches, under torture, likewise eventually confessed.

James, in the meanwhile, fuming whatever growing impatience at the vacillation of his council, waited at Craigmillar Castle for news of what was taking place. Summoning Sir James Melville and his brother Robert, he asked them for their advice on how to treat the Danish noblemen who were thought, at that moment, to be still upon the sea, sailing for Scotland with Queen Anne.

According to Melville, the chancellor, Maitland, aware that he was out of favour with the King, volunteered himself to sail to Norway to bring her back to Scotland. But, be that as it may, other sources tell that James asked Francis Bothwell, as Lord High Admiral, for an estimate on what a full embassy, sent to Norway, would cost. The result was so exorbitant that James, who was always short of money and careful with the little he had, decided that it would be, not only cheaper, but more expedient, to fetch Anne from Norway himself. Bothwell, meanwhile, as one of the King's closest relations, was to remain in Scotland to take part in the government, together with the chancellor, the latter being much put out by the appointment of Sir Robert Melville as vice-chancellor during his Majesty's absence abroad.

Four ships in all sailed from Scotland over the North Sea. The weather was rough, it now being late autumn, the last part of the voyage proving perilous in the extreme. Nevertheless King James landed safely at Tonsberg from where he travelled overland to Oslo, where, without waiting to change his clothes, he rushed into the palace of King Christian IV, boots and all.

On 23 November, the marriage took place in the hall of the old Bishop's palace, before the newlywed couple, travelled across land to Denmark where, in the Palace of Kronborg, James and Anne spent the rest of the winter before, as the weather calmed down, they were able to put out to sea.

On 1 May they landed safely at Leith. With them came Peter Munk, the admiral of Denmark, he who by a cuff to the ear of the bailie of Copenhagen had ignited the death dealing storms, but who now, following the Queen's coronation, was rewarded with medals and golden chains. After six days the royal couple proceeded to Holyrood. James and the nobles on horseback and Anne in a Danish coach richly adorned with cloth of gold and purple velvet and pulled by eight horses. On 17 May she was crowned in the Abbey Kirk in a ceremony lasting seven hours. Following this to the sound of trumpets and beating of drums and guns thundering from the castle, she made a formal entrance into Edinburgh. The King was entranced with her. Only later would their lack of shared interests, and Anne's conversion to Catholicism, gradually drive them apart.

James VI as a boy aged eight with hawk on wrist. Scottish National Portrait Gallery Edinburgh.

By Arnold Bronckorst

Mary I Queen of Scotland (1542-1587)

John Erskine, Earl of Mar S.N.P.G.

Courtesy of Project Gutenberg

John Douglas, Earl of Morton. S.N.P.G.

By Arnold Bronckorst

Esme Stewart, Sieur d'Aubigny, Duke of Lennox. S.N.P.G.

Anne of Denmark by Marcus Gheeraerts

Princess Elizabeth, later 'The Winter Queen' of Bohemia,
miniature by Nicholas Hilliard

Guy Fawkes

Linlithgow Palace

Holyrood Palace

Edinburgh Castle

Stirling Castle

CHAPTER 18

By Poison or Witchcraft – To Kill or Kidnap the King

Hardly had James returned from Denmark before his chancellor, Maitland, with whom he was now on better terms, had induced three of the most troublesome of the chiefs of the Western Isles, namely MacLean of Duart, MacDonald of Islay and Donald Gorm of Sleat, to come to Edinburgh to verify the charters through which, in a rather dubious context, they held their land from the crown. Arriving to a most unpleasant surprise, they found themselves warded in Edinburgh Castle. Forced to stand trial on a charge of treason, they bribed their way out by repaying their creditors, but did not pay the 20,000 merks annually demanded for property over which they had no security, which was due to the King. Hostages held for the payment were kept in Blackness Castle on the Forth, but soon released, so that while the chiefs obtained charters for their property, hitherto held by the sword, the 20,000 merks, owed to the Scottish Exchequer, was never paid.

Another prisoner in Edinburgh Castle was the Earl of Bothwell, charged together with the Earl of Huntly and others for engaging in an armed uprising to plot and seize the King at Holyrood Palace. Bothwell surrendered himself on 11th May 1589 and together with his accomplices, was tried, on 24 May. All were found guilty but had their sentences deferred subject to the King's mercy.

Then two years later, on 15 April 1591, Bothwell was arrested again on the capital charge of witchcraft. Accused of trying to cause the King's death by sorcery, he was imprisoned in Edinburgh Castle, this time with the strong likelihood of facing death.

The accusations stemmed from those of the Danish admiral, Peter Munk, attributing the storms, which had so nearly wrecked the ship in which Queen Anne had sailed from Denmark, to sorcery. In July 1590 a number of women termed witches, in that country, had been arrested. They included one called Anna Koldings, who under torture divulged the names of five other women, one of them being none other than Mail, wife of the burgomaster of Copenhagen. All confessed that they had been guilty of sorcery in raising storms that threatened Queen Anne's voyage and that it was they who had sent the devils running up and down the keel of her ship. In September, on the news that two women had been burnt as witches at Kronborg, James decided to set up his own tribunal.

Then one of those accused in Scotland, a mid-wife called Agnes Sampson, declared that the devil had shown her a picture of James VI saying he should be: 'consumed at the instance of a noble man Francis Eral Bodowell.' Afterwards, again at their meeting by night in the Kirk of North Berwick, the devil, clad in a black gown, with a black hat upon his head appeared. He preached to a great number of them out of the pulpit, having lit candles round about him. The effect of his language was to know what hurt they had done, how many they had gained to their opinion since their last meeting, and what success the melting of the picture had, and such vain toys. And because an old, silly, poor ploughman, called Gray Meill, chanced to say that nothing ailed the King yet, God be thanked, the Devil gave him a great blow. Then divers among them entered in reasoning, marvelling that all their devilry could do no harm to the King, as it had done to other divers. The devil answered, "Il est un home de Dieu." Certainly he is a man of God, and does no wrong wittingly, but is inclined to all godliness, justice and virtue; therefore God hath preserved him in the midst of many dangers. Now, after the devil had ended his admonitions, he came down out of the pulpit, and caused all the company to kiss his arse; which they said was like cold ice; his body was hard as iron, as they thought who handled him; his face was terrible, his nose like the beak of an eagle; great burning eyes; his hands and his legs were hairy, with claws upon his hands and feet like the griffin; he spoke with a hollow voice.

But it was a man called Ritchie Graham, described as 'a Westland man who had a familiar spirit, the which Ritchie they said could both do and tell many things, chiefly against the Earl of Bothwell,' who confessed to conspiring with the earl, which actually prompted Bothwell's arrest in April 1591. According to Melville:

'the said Ritchie was apprehended and brought to Edinburgh, and being examined before His Majesty, I being present, he granted that he had a familiar spirit, which showed him sundry things; but he denied that he was a witch, or had any frequentation with them. But when it was answered to him again how that Annie Sampsoun had declared that he caused the Earl of Bothwell address him to her, he granted that to be true, and that the Earl of Bothwell had knowledge of him by Effie Mackalloun and Barbara Napier, Edinburgh women. Whereupon he was sent for by the Earl of Bothwell, who required his help to cause the King's Majesty his master to like well of him. And to that effect he gave the earl some drug or herb, willing him at some convenient time to touch therewith His Majesty's face. Which being done by the said Earl, and found him not the better, he dealt again with the said Ritchie to get His Majesty wrecked, as Ritchie alleged, who said that he could not do such things himself, but that a notable midwife who was a witch, called Annie Sampson, could bring any such purpose to pass. Thus far, the said Ritchie Graham affirmed diver's times before the council, nevertheless he was burnt, with the said Sampson and other witches. This, Ritchie alleged that it is certain of the fairy folk; and that spirits may take a form, and be seen, though not felt.'

But who were they, these witches and devils who, during the sixteenth and seventeenth centuries, throughout the length and breadth of Scotland, kept men, women and children alike, living in mortal fear?

Down the Firth of Forth they came, bobbing about on their sieves, so the story runs. Very soon more than a hundred suspected witches were arrested in North Berwick. They held their covens on the Aulde Kirk Green, now part of the present day harbour. Many confessed to having met with the Devil in the church at night, and devoted themselves to doing evil, including poisoning the King and members of his household and attempting to sink the King's ship.[59]

125

Amongst them the two most significant were the aforementioned Agnes Sampson, described in this instance as 'a respected and elderly woman from Humbie in what then was Haddingtonshire and is now East Lothian, and Doctor John Fian a schoolmaster and scholar in Prestonpans. Both refused adamantly to confess and were put to severe torture. Sampson, when eventually brought before King James and a council of nobles, did finally confess. Having done so, the wretched woman was fastened to the wall of her cell by a witch's bridle, an iron instrument with four sharp prongs forced into her mouth, so that two prongs pressed against the tongue, and two others against the cheeks, kept without sleep, with a rope thrown round her head, she died, it would seem from sheer exhaustion, owning up to no less than fifty-three indictments against her. Finally, she was strangled and burnt as a witch.

Doctor Fian, described as 'a notable sorcerer, confessed to attending a Sabbath with no less than two hundred witches. Tortured in the most agonising way, his fingernails extracted and then having pins thrust therein before being subjected both to the pilliwinks, (pillory?) and the boot, a medieval contraption by which nails were driven into a leg encased in a boot, he was finally taken to the Castlehill in Edinburgh, where, on 16 December, he was burned at the stake.

Meanwhile, the Earl of Bothwell, held in ward in Edinburgh Castle, managed to escape over the wall and reach Caithness. But there he was pursued by what Melville described as 'malcontents' who easily cajoled him into a plot to kidnap the King and kill Maitland, the chancellor.

They acted swiftly once the plan was made. Bothwell, with James Douglas, a man described as 'sometime laird of Spott,' the laird of Niddry and one John Colville, together with some others, made their way into Holyrood Palace by means of a passage through an old stable about which one of them knew. Once in the building they cried, 'Justice, justice, a Bothwell! A Bothwell!' and made for the King's chamber. Some of them ran up the stair but as they did so the laird of Spott heard shouts coming from the guard-room, where some of his men were detained and leaving his companions, he set off to try to set them free.

Sir Robert Melville, Master of the Household, was having supper with the chancellor when he heard the sound of shouts and clash of arms. Both of them ran to their respective chambers, where, making use of the furniture, they barricaded themselves safely behind doors. Meanwhile Bothwell, John Colville and others, by this time having climbed the stairs, were hammering against the door of the Queen's chamber wherein they believed the King to be. Harry Lindsay of Kilfaurs, Master of her Household, gallantly defended the entrance until the assailants, having resorted to sledge hammers and fire brought by John Colville, succeeded in breaking it down. But even as it crashed open they found the room empty: the King having dashed upstairs to the tower on the floor immediately above.

As all this was happening, the chancellor, while defending his door himself, ordered his men to shoot out of the windows and through doors where Robert Scot, brother of the laird of Balweary, received a bullet through the thigh. More damage might have been done had not Sir Robert Melville, Master of the Household, that was newly planted on the north side of the close, shouted to Maitland not to shoot towards that side. Maitland, hearing his voice, took courage and at the same time the intended murderers fled.

Sir James Melville and the Duke of Lennox, sitting at supper when all the commotion began, also fortified the doors and stairs with all the furniture they could find. Then, as the noise abated, Lennox, looking out of the window, saw a company of his own men gathered within the close. Sword in hand, he ran after Bothwell who, with his confederates, jumped onto fast horses to escape into the darkness of the night. But such was the force of his fury at the abject failure of his plan, that meeting John Shaw, the Master Stabler to the King, he slew both him and his brother, for nothing other than spite.

It is indicative of the King's courage, that, after what must have been a sleepless night, he insisted on going hunting. Sir Robert Melville, jumped out of bed and wearing only his shirt and nightgown, rushed to the door to grab his horse's bridle while pleading with him not to risk his life. James, however, ignored him although he did condescend to retire into what Melville called 'the town of Edinburgh' for his greater safety. Nonetheless the threats against his life and plots to capture him continued, making it necessary for him to be not only constantly guarded but to stay within his lodging at night.

Bothwell was lying low. But reports of his being at his mother's house at Morham and at Coldingham sent James off, determined to track him down. It was on 13 January 1592 (Gregorian calendar) that the King led a party eastwards out of Holyrood in the direction of Haddington where Bothwell had last been reported as having been seen. The roads were probably slippery and it may have been Friday 13[th,] but whatever the unpropitious circumstances, the King's horse slipped and threw him into a pool of water from which a local farmer pulled him out 'by the necke'.

Returning to Edinburgh, after his rather undignified rescue, James found a letter from Bothwell, addressed to the Clergy of Edinburgh, indignantly denying the charges of witchcraft levelled against him.

The next that was heard of this tiresome cousin was that he was in Dundee. The Privy Council denounced some of his henchmen, amongst them Ross of Banagowan, the Master of Gray, and his brother Robert, for assisting him before, on 7 April, James set out again to capture him, crossing the Forth by the Queensferry to the Fife shore. It proved to be a wasted journey. No doubt warned by his spies of the King's coming, there was no sign of Bothwell in Dundee.

However, the hand of the law was heavy, for when the Scottish Parliament convened, on 5 June 1592, for the first time after nearly five years, Bothwell was stripped of all his titles, honours and lands. Predictably it was like putting flame to the fire. On 28 June, when it was just getting light, between one and two in the morning, Bothwell, at the head of about 300 men tried to capture Falkland Palace wherein, he knew the King to be staying.

But James, himself, had been forewarned and together with the Queen and his attendants, had taken refuge in the tower of the palace, locking the door securely from within. Frustrated, Bothwell withdrew, no doubt wasting the land as he left, but looking for safety he fled. On 29 and 30 June, proclamations were sent out, both for his own arrest and that of his accomplices, including, Martine of Cardone, Lumsden of Airdrie and Scott of Balwearie, brother of the man, who at Holyrood, had received a bullet in the thigh.

But Bothwell once more had vanished, eluding all pursuit, and the attempt to capture him was abandoned during the first week of August. Nonetheless, by this time, the crown had got possession of all his houses and lands and imprisoned some of his supporters, George Keith, the Earl Marischal, Lord Home and Sinclair of Roslyn amongst them.

On 14 September the Privy Council proclaimed an order for an armed muster to join the King in Teviotdale in pursuit of the outlawed rebels. James left Edinburgh for Dalkeith on 9 October and proceeded to Jedburgh. But again his prey had vanished into the Border hills.

The next thing known of Bothwell, is that in January of the following year of 1593, he was in the north of England being feted by his English friends. On 7 June a much aggrieved King James asked Queen Elizabeth to return him to Scotland without any further delay.

That the Queen complied or Bothwell himself decided to risk it, remains unknown. Attainted by Act of Parliament, on 21 July, he promptly showed his defiance. Three days later, with the aid of his mother, the formidable Jane Hepburn, Mistress of Caithness, and his sister, the Countess of Atholl, he somehow got into Holyroodhouse, presumably through the passage from the stable, or another one of which he knew.

Once there, he forced himself into the King's bedroom, where, as some of his friends, hands on the hilts of their swords, joined him, the King—terrified as he certainly was—accepted his sworn vows of loyalty and agreed to his pardon being made.[60]

On Friday 10 August 1593, after what is described as 'a farcical trial' on the old charge of witchcraft, Bothwell was acquitted. The King, however, once freed of the threat of physical violence, conspired with the Earl's enemies, headed by the Chancellor Sir John Maitland, to rescind on his pardon. Messengers were sent to meet him at Linlithgow, where, on 7 September, he was informed that James intended to allow his pardon only if he would voluntarily go into exile. That he did not intend to do this became evident when, early in October, a party of his supporters, including the Earls of Montrose, Atholl, and Gowrie, were seen mustering in the vicinity of Linlithgow. The expected rising did not happen but, on 11 October a warrant was issued against Bothwell and his known confederates, and on them failing to appear as summoned, all were proclaimed rebels on 25th of the month.

The winter passed uneventfully until, on 2 April 1594, a fracas took place between the King's army and Bothwell's 'fiery tail,' below Arthur's Seat between Edinburgh and Leith. It proved to be merely a skirmish. The King retired to the Burgh Moor (Colinton today) while Bothwell retreated, first to Dalkeith and then to his own lands on the Scottish Borders.

On 30 September 1594, with the Privy Council, once more calling him a rebel, Francis Bothwell decided to abandon his Presbyterian religion and ally himself to the Catholic Earls of Huntly, Angus and Errol in rebellion against the King.

CHAPTER 19

Poison, Rebellion and Banishment – Death in Many Forms

James had survived the Ruthvens and the witches but always there was the unseen danger, the assassin's knife behind the tapestries, and the even more insidious threat of poison, then, so frequently used. Like most men of rank he had tasters, employed to eat the first bit of meat or slice of bread, but few of them ever fell dead. Poison was so easy to administer, Lord Leicester was only one of the many believed to have killed several people by its use.

One victim of this particularly vile mode of destruction was Archibald Campbell, the young, 7th Earl of Argyll, who, poisoned by bribed servants in Edinburgh, was almost done to death in this way. He did eventually recover but only thanks to a strong constitution, which proved to be the saviour of his life.

James could trust no one. Existing evidence proves that even his chancellor, John Maitland of Thirlestane, brother of his mother's most trusted secretary William Maitland of Lethington, was in league with a coterie of Highland lords who bound themselves, in a most solemn manner, to encompass, by every means in their power, the destruction of James, Earl of Moray, Archibald, Earl of Argyll, Colin Campbell of Lundy, Argyll's only brother and heir apparent, and John Campbell Earl of Calder. While the actual expedition of the murders was to be carried out by the Highlanders; Huntly, Maitland and Lord Maxwell, (alias the Earl of Morton) pledged themselves to defend them from any consequences that might occur.

The evil genius behind Argyll's destruction was the man commonly known as Black Duncan of the Cowl, Duncan Campbell, 7th laird of Glenorchy, who aspired with Campbell of Lochnell (who in the event of Argyll and his brother dying childless, would inherit Argyll's land and his titles) to destroy him. Following the successful outcome of their connivance, Lochnell agreed to give the lands of Pincarton in Stirlingshire, belonging to Argyll, to the chancellor, while the Lordship of Lorn and the lands of Benderloch, would go to Black Duncan of Glenorchy, who would thus acquire the leadership of Clan Campbell.

Glenorchy had quarrelled with Campbell of Calder over his giving shelter to some of the Clan MacGregor, with whom he was currently in dispute over possession of land. He was therefore behind the conspiracy which, on 4 February 1592, resulted in Campbell of Calder being murdered by a hired assassin, armed with a hagbut, who shot him through a lighted window of a house on Loch Feochan, near Oban. Then it was Moray's turn to die. [61]

The King loved the Earl of Huntly, the dashing young nobleman whose great love of hunting he shared. Married to a sister of Ludovic Duke of Lennox, and having agreed, hypocritically to become a Protestant, James made him captain of the guard, lodging him in his own rooms. Yet detesting violence as he did, the King's attachment to Huntly seems strange in view of the fact of his reputation - he was known to be both treacherous and cruel. The turrets of his castle of Strathbogie were bestrewed with the severed heads and limbs of his victims and famously, having captured two cooks from an enemy clan, he had ordered them roasted alive.

The vendetta between the Earl of Huntly and the Earl of Moray sprang from a long nourished hatred, descending from the time when Mary Queen of Scots, had given the rich earldom of Moray to her half-brother, Lord James Stewart (subsequently, following her imprisonment, Regent of Scotland) in defiance of Huntly who claimed the land to be his own. The 6th Earl of Argyll had thereafter consistently supported Moray in the on-going disputes, for no better reason than that he had married, Agnes Keith, (daughter of the Earl Marischal) widow of the Regent.

The Countess of Argyll, by her first marriage, had three daughters, the eldest of whom, in 1581, had married James Stewart, 2nd Lord Doune, who had then assumed, *jure uxoris*, the title of the Earl of Moray.

Meanwhile George, Earl of Huntly, waited for a chance to win revenge. It came in 1592 when, Huntly, knowing that Bothwell was now an outlaw, persuaded the King to give him a commission of fire and sword to 'pursue the Earl of Bothwell and all his partakers.'

It was Andrew Stewart, Lord Ochiltree, who, persuaded Moray to come to his own house of Donibristle on the Fife coast, for what was supposed to be a consultation. It is claimed that Ochiltree, warned of an impending attack, was actually on his way to protect him, with an escort of fifty men, when stopped by a messenger from the King who ordered him to turn back.

So was James privy to the horror that was about to take place? Or was he simply bent on Huntly capturing Bothwell, the constant threat to his safety and object of his commission, by any possible means?

On 7 February, it was growing dark at Donibristle, when Huntly rode up to the gates at the head of forty armed men. Captain John Gordon of Gight, advancing with the royal warrant (issued for the capture of Bothwell), demanded Moray to surrender in the King's name. Moray refused, and Gordon, picked out by a sharp-shooter on the castle walls, pitched forward, wounded, onto his face. The Gordons, naturally incensed, then contrived to set the castle on fire. Through suffocating smoke, the Sheriff of Moray, rushed out to try and cause a diversion, but was quickly overcome and killed. Then Moray himself made a dash for it, running down to the shore. He might well have escaped but the tassel, in what is generally called his night cap, but which was actually the cloth cover of his helmet, had caught a spark and the 'Bonny Earl' was betrayed by what looked like a fire-fly, as he scrambled along the shingle, running for his life. The Gordons, catching him, fell on him without mercy, stabbing him many times. "You have spoiled a better face than you own," were his last words, gasped out traditionally to Huntly, but evidence suggests that it was probably William Gordon of Gight, whose brother had just been shot, who dealt him the fatal wound.

The Catholic conspiracies continued. In the winter of 1592-3 a Scottish Catholic, George Ker was arrested as he was about to sail for Spain. On his person were found mysterious sheets of blank paper signed at the bottom by Huntly, Errol, Angus and Sir

Patrick Gordon of Auchindoun. Tortured by the boot, Ker confessed. The plot had begun with Father William Crichton, a Scottish Jesuit in Spain, who believed that King Philip would send an army to Scotland if assured of Scottish support. The Earls had taken the precaution of sending the blank documents to be later filled in by Ker and Crichton.

This was going too far even for the King, whose own position was enhanced by the birth of his heir, Prince Henry, at Stirling Castle on 19^t February 1594. The news brought a surge of joy to the people who, according to a contemporary 'went daft with mirth.' But the ministers of the Kirk still demanded the Earl's punishment and to pacify them, in the following June, the three Catholic Earls of Huntly, Errol and Angus, and the other Catholics accused of plotting with Philip of Spain for the restoration of the Catholic religion in Scotland, were forfeited by Parliament.

Huntly, by setting free some Catholics imprisoned by the magistrates of Aberdeen, then gave the King a reason to commission the young Earl of Argyll, whom he knew to be Huntly's enemy, the Earl of Atholl and Lord Forbes, to march against the rebels and hopefully reduce them to obedience.

Argyll, who was only eighteen and quite recently recovered from the attempt on his life made by his servants bribed to poison him, was apparently in ignorance that the man behind it was none other than Archibald Campbell of Lochnell, at that time heir apparent to his earldom. Lochnell, by hereditary right, was commander of one of the divisions of his army.

Having raised a force of six or seven thousand men from his own and other clans, Argyll marched into Badenoch and laid siege to the castle of Ruthven, which gallantly held by the Macphersons, defied his attempts at capture. He then moved on towards Strathbogie, determined to lay waste to Huntly's lands. However, upon approaching Glenlivat, he found that both Huntly and Errol, with a combined force of fourteen to fifteen hundred men, most of them cavalry, were waiting to confront him. Trusting his superiority in numbers, Argyll with confidence, awaited a confrontation. Acting on the defensive, he took up a strong position, totally unaware that Lochnell, had told Huntly to fire at his banner, easily distinguishable by the bright yellow of its colour.

Lochnell had arranged his own doom, for as Huntly's guns blazed forth, it was not Argyll who fell but Lochnell, caught by what must have been the ricochet of a cannon ball, which killed him outright.

During the following confusion, Huntly, with his cavalry charged. Many fell on both sides but despite the heroic fighting of the MacLeans, under their chief Lachlan MacLean of Duart, Argyll's army was defeated.

Argyll himself left the field to ride at great speed to Dundee where he knew the King to be. James admonished him, but then himself led a strong army to defeat the rebellious earls. Huntly's castles of Strathbogie and Slaines were demolished, while the lords and lairds who had followed him were forfeited and their estates divided amongst the royalists.

James, however, was merciful to the leaders, unwilling to entirely destroy the power of the Catholic chiefs who were his best defence against the over-riding Protestant government with which he had to contend. Also, most fervently, he wished to avoid annoying the English Catholics, thus impeding his likely accession to Queen Elizabeth's throne. The English monarch herself was furious, demanding that the Catholic earls be punished with the utmost severity. 'Clap up the Earls' she advised him 'and teach them how a King deals with treason!' But James, loving Huntly as he did, was determined to be lenient, allowing both him and Errol to escape abroad and Angus to the wilds of his own land of Douglasdale.

Francis Bothwell, does not appear to have been actively involved in the rebellion of the Catholic Earls, but his brother Hercules, captured by John Colville and William Hume, who promised him his life, was then hanged, to howls of sympathy from the populace, at the market place in Edinburgh.[62]

On the same day, 18 February 1595, with the King's pardon revoked, a new sentence of treason was issued against Bothwell. He managed to escape capture by hiding in Caithness and the Isles of Orkney but eventually sailed to France from Newhaven to land in Normandy. King James, on hearing this, sent a special message to the French King Henry IV asking for Bothwell to be extradited, a request which Henry refused. Subsequently Bothwell left France for Spain, by now a soldier of fortune looking for any employment he could find. He was rumoured to be in London having crossed the Channel from Dieppe. James was told of his being there with John Colville in 1598 but did not believe it to be true. However, it must have been more than a rumour because Sir Walter Raleigh advised Queen Elizabeth to get rid of him, telling her that he 'will ever be the canker of her estate and safety.'[63]

Bothwell must then have left England for he is next known to have been living in poverty in Naples, where he died, aged fifty, in November 1612, apparently devastated by the news of the death of King James's eldest son, Prince Henry, the Prince of Wales, whom he believed would grant him a pardon to allow him to come home. Impoverished to the point of near destitution, he was nonetheless given a magnificent funeral by the Spanish Viceroy of Naples, Pedro Fernández de Castro y Andrade.

CHAPTER 20
Financial and Ecclesiastical Control

The death of the chancellor, Sir John Maitland of Lethington, in October 1595, gave the King the chance to take a tighter hold of the government and the office of chancellor being vacant during the next three years, to forcefully direct his own policies.

He began by issuing a proclamation that as his subjects 'King and Sovereign Lord,' he will be obeyed and reverenced as a king. He will execute his power and authority against whatsoever persons, be they nobles, councillors or servants, who shall 'contemn his Highness, his authority or laws.'

However, once in control of his government King James became ever more aware that it was money, or rather the lack of it, that was the real cause of his failure to control the lawlessness that so bedevilled his land. Upon enquiry he found the state of his finances to be worse than he had previously realised them to be. Impoverished from the start of his reign, by the 1590s, James was reduced to such poverty that even his own household was maintained from the income of their own rents of his officers of state.

The reasons for this could be traced back to his immediate ancestors, his mother and before her his grandfather James V. Dependent on the goodwill of the great lords to enforce their power, they had ceded them lands and benefices, including possession as commendators of some of the rich abbeys, owning some of the best agricultural acres in Scotland thus robbing the royal treasury of the income it should have acquired. Consequently, in debt to moneylenders as well as to his own peers, James, in desperation, resorted to debasing the coinage and purloining the mint.

On examining the sources of his income, following Maitland's death, James discovered that the offices of the exchequer were lining their own pockets at the expense of the crown. It was at this moment that Queen Anne's councillors, who had been handling her finances with proven success, offered both to administer the King's revenues and to provide him with enough ready money to maintain his existing estate. The climax came when, on the New Year's Day of 1596, the Queen's Council presented her with a purse containing no less than a thousand pounds in gold. Triumphantly, dangling the glinting coins beneath his nose, she offered half of it to her husband and asked him when his Council would give him as much?

Convinced now of chicanery, James instantly dismissed the Treasurer, the Earl of Glamis and his fellow exchequer officials and appointed Anne's councillors as a board to control his finances in their place.

The eight councillors, known for their number as the Octavians, were soon to prove their efficiency. All of them competent men, they included Walter Stewart, who educated with James at Stirling was later to become Lord Treasurer, Alexander Seton, Lord Urquhart, President of the Court of Session, who, as the Earl of Dunfermline, would later become Lord Chancellor, John Lindsay, Parson of Menmuir, described by Spottiswoode 'as a man of exquisite learning,' James Elphinstone, later Lord Balmerino, who took office as Secretary, and finally Tomas Hamilton, or 'Tam o' the Cowgate,' as James called him from the part of Edinburgh where he lived.

The Octavians held great power, the King drawing up a document to give them control of all the royal revenue and binding himself to abide by their judgement. Thanks to them the royal finances were all too briefly stabilised before being eclipsed by a new clash between Church and State.

The trouble arose when the Earls of Huntly and Errol returned to Scotland in the summer of 1596. James could not afford to antagonise the Catholics, believing as he did that his hopes of succession to the English throne lay largely in the support of the still strong Catholic faction in both England and Scotland as well as on the Continent. It was to this purpose that, in August 1596, he wrung from the convention of the estates at Falkland a concession that if the Earls satisfied both the King and the Kirk, they should be allowed to stay in Scotland.

The Kirk reacted in fury. Andrew Melville, a well-known zealot for all that he was the uncle of the diplomat Sir James, who appeared uninvited at the conference of Falkland, hurled insults at the entire assembly, calling them traitors for submitting to the return of the Catholic Earls.

Then a month later, in October, Melville returned to Falkland, when, grabbing the King by the sleeve, he so famously called him 'God's silly vassal', assuring him that he was brought into extreme danger both of his life and crown, and said, "With you, the country and Kirk of Christ is like to wreck. And therefore, Sir, I must tell you, there are two Kings and two Kingdoms in Scotland. There is Christ Jesus the King and his kingdom the Kirk, whose subject King James the Sixth is and of whose Kingdom is not King nor a head, but a member!"

The assembled company listened, holding their breaths in expectation of Melville's immediate arrest. But amazingly, James listened and, at the end of the minister's diatribe, promised that the Catholic Earls should obtain no grace from him until they had satisfied the Kirk.

The emergency seemed to be over, but respite proved to be brief. A scandalous sermon was preached by David Black, minister of St Andrews, who, declaring Queen Elizabeth an atheist, warned that English bishops had induced the King to impose episcopal government in Scotland. The King himself, he claimed, had known that the Catholic Earls were coming home, but what could be expected when Satan ruled the court and, in the council, when judges and councillors were cormorants and men of no religion, when the Queen of Scotland was a woman for whom, for fashion's sake, the clergy might pray, but from whom no good could be hoped. 'Were not all kings devil's bairns?'[64]

This was too much even for James who, by ignoring the insults of Melville, believed that he had done all in his power to placate the Protestant extremists. Black was called before the council but refused its jurisdiction, claiming that he had the right to face trial only before an ecclesiastical court. His fate hung in the balance while some malicious courtiers, jealous of the power of the Octavians, informed the Edinburgh ministers that the party planned their ruin. Violent, inflammatory sermons in St Giles led to a riot. Citizens brandishing axes ran to the tolbooth where they knew the King to be. To cries of 'bring forth the wicked Hamam', they thundered the blades against the door.

But the Provost calmed the people, and an escort of loyal men protected James as he hurried down the Canongate to the safety of Holyrood Palace. Next day, he moved to the still greater security of Linlithgow Palace from where he returned to Edinburgh, leading a band of fierce, well-armed Border reivers, at sight of which the rebellious ministers left their pulpits and fled.

James had scored a personal triumph but for the sake of securing the support of the Catholics in Scotland, he found himself forced to dismiss the Octavians as controllers of his financial affairs.

His decision, although causing him personal chagrin, proved his knowledge of statesmanship, which, despite the derision of his critics, he was steadily coming to acquire. The zealots were defeated, while in the Kirk itself, a more moderate party, satisfied by his handling of the recent perilous situation, saw the wisdom of supporting him while the King, for his part, was learning to manipulate the General Assemblies. First from one held in Perth in February 1597 and then from another in Dundee in the following May, he achieved important concessions. Ministers swore to be more prudent in the words that they preached and above all, to avoid political controversy. Commissioners chosen to deal with the Catholic Earls received them into the Kirk at Aberdeen. Then, following this, an act was passed ensuring that those ministers, appointed by the King as bishops and other clerics, must be bona-fide clergymen and that their position in the Kirk should henceforth be decided by both the King and the General Assembly.

It was James's intention in this respect, namely to establish an aristocratic first estate, appointed by himself at the suggestion of a concourse of the Scottish nobles, that was thus put forward in his book the *Basilikon Doron,* written in secret in the summer of 1598. Andrew Melville, who somehow managed to see a manuscript copy, tried furiously to suppress its publication but without success. A year later, James appointed three diocesan bishops to the seas of Caithness, Ross and Aberdeen unaware that in accomplishing his personal triumph, he was sowing the seed of discord that would later plague the reign of his as yet unborn younger son.

CHAPTER 21
Rebellion

It was in the spring of 1596 that a notorious cattle thief, known as Kinmount Willie, imprisoned in Carlisle Castle awaiting execution for his numerous crimes, was saved by Sir Walter Scott, Lord of Buccleuch and the keeper of Liddesdale, who, under cover of darkness, raided the castle, rescued him and carried him back to Scotland.

The Scots were jubilant. Queen Elizabeth was predictably furious demanding the imprisonment of Buccleuch who was, for a short time, held at St Andrews. James then did his best to placate her by going down to the Borders to hang as many of the cattle rustlers as could be caught, thereby strengthening his authority, before, on his daughter being born at Dunfermline in August, he named the fair-haired baby Elizabeth in deference to the Queen.

James had won control over the Borders, but was under no delusions of the threat to his rule in the Highlands where clan feuds continued unabated in the ferocity of a lawless land. Under no illusions as to what was happening in a part of his kingdom as yet beyond any effectual form of control, he summed up the situation accurately in his own words:

"Furthermore, as for the Highlands, I shortly comprehend them all in two sorts of people: the one that dwelleth in our mainland that are barbarous for the most part and yet mixed with some show of civility," but the people of the Western Isles, he described as 'wolves and wild boars.' [65]

That feuding amongst the clans of the Highlands and the Western Isles was indigenous, the King was only too well aware. It was during the previous month, of July 1596, when he was holding his council at Dunfermline that a young man, wearing the Highland dress of a kilt and plaid in one piece, threw himself at his feet. He proved to be Alasdair MacGregor of Glenstrae, who, 'in maist humble manner, acknowledging his offences and disobedience bypast, whereof he maist earnestly repent it', pledged himself, as chief, that he and his clan would keep good rule in the country and be answerable to his Majesty and to justice.

It was now seven years since Drummond-Ernoch, the King's Keeper of the royal forest of Glenartney and the Steward of Strathearn, had ridden out into the forest to find venison for the great feast planned to celebrate the King's return from Denmark with his bride. Unfortunately, he had been alone when three or four of the Clan MacGregor, resentful because he had hanged some of their men for poaching, had set upon him and killed him. Bearing his head, they had reached the house of Ardvoirlich on the south side of Loch Earn, where lived their victim's sister, married to the Stewart laird. Demanding hospitality, as was customary in the Highlands, they were let into the house where they left the head of Drummond-Ernoch on the dining room table with a lump of cheese stuffed into its mouth. Mrs Stewart, demented at the sight of it, fled into the hills, where her husband found her shortly before their child, a son, was born.

Repercussions had been immediate, but Alasdair, chief of the MacGregors of Glenstrae, a young man of just twenty-one at the time, had summoned the whole of Clan Gregor to meet in the little graveyard at Balquidder where the severed head of Drummond-Ernoch was set on one of the tombstones. Approaching, Alasdair had laid his hand upon it, swearing to take the blood guilt on his own head and never reveal the names of the murderers. One by one, his clansmen had then followed him, each placing his hand on the head, while repeating the oath of their chief.

In Edinburgh the news of what had happened had caused such a furore that, on 3 February 1590, the council had outlawed and condemned to death the whole of Clan Gregor for the murder of Drummond-Ernoch. A commission had been issued to the Earls of Huntly, Atholl and the guardians of the young Argyll, authorising them 'to seek, take, and apprehend' Alasdair MacGregor of Glenstrae, together with all the others of Clan Gregor or their assisters, culpable of the said odious murder, or of theft, reset of theft, hership and sorning.' They were to be tried at a special assize held on the spot, and if found guilty were to be executed immediately, their possessions going half to the State and half to the person who had apprehended them.[66]

Sir Duncan Campbell of Glenorchy, for long at feud with the MacGregors in his neighbouring strath of Glenstrae, then saw his chance and quickly applied for legal authority to evict the clan from the lands they had held for centuries with the power of the sword but without the legal charter needed to prove their rights. Alasdair, in defiance, had continued to hold Glenstrae, but, with the murder of Campbell of Calder, who had allowed some of the MacGregors to live on his land, he lost his best friend. It was thus, for this reason, that the young chief of Glenstrae, took the risk of being immediately arrested, when, in July 1596, at Dunfermline, he threw himself at the mercy of the King.

James was known to be lenient, detesting bloodshed as he did. Nonetheless, the members of the council were most surprised, and none more than Alasdair himself, when it was decreed that Alasdair should remain himself as a hostage for the good behaviour of his people. Even more extraordinary, he was not to be kept in ward. Instead, he was to be in his Majesty's company and house and not to depart without the King's license and letter; and thereupon he swore his oath to be faithful as 'the King's household-man,' and 'as he should answer to God upon the salvation of his soul.'[67]

Immediately afterwards a new pardon was issued to Alasdair and all his followers, formally acquitting them of all guilt of the murder of Drummond-Ernoch, and 'for all other (crimes) committed by the said Alexander or by any other of the surname of MacGregor.'

Alasdair was not the only man held hostage for his people's good behaviour. Another was Sir James MacDonald of Dunyveg in Islay, held at the King's court from 1592, who the King had specifically knighted, in proof of his personal friendship for a very likeable young man. The MacDonalds had long been at feud with the MacLeans of Duart on Mull, mostly on account of possession of the Rinns of Islay, on the island's south-west coast, which the MacDonalds claimed to possess. The enmity between the two clans, which had lasted for many years, had resulted in great brutality on both sides.

In 1596 King James issued a licence to Sir James of Dunyveg, to visit his father, Angus MacDonald, in the hopes of his making a submission to the authority of the crown. [68] In this he was successful to the point that his father did come to Edinburgh to receive a pardon in the following year. This was granted on the condition of his firstly finding security for the arrears of his crown rents, which had been allowed to accumulate to a large amount of money, secondly to remove his clan and defenders from Kintyre in mainland Argyll, and the Rinns of Islay and lastly to surrender his castle of Dunyveg in Islay, before 20 May, to the person whom the King should send to receive it. None of these specifications were met and in 1598, the King, for a second time, sent Sir James MacDonald to reason with his father.

This time Sir James was taking no chances. Reaching his father's house of Askomull, (near the present town of Campbeltown in Kintyre) where he knew both his parents to be, in the dead of night he surrounded it with two or three hundred armed men. Then loudly, as he shouted to his father to surrender, he was met by a blank refusal, voiced with a proliferation of oaths. Prepared for this to happen—it was typical of his father's behaviour—he told his men to push their flaming torches below the thatch. The house became an inferno before Angus, badly burned, made a dash from the door to be seized by his son's men. Carried to Smerbie in Kintyre, he was made a prisoner held in irons.

Following this, Sir James received a letter from the King expressing his approval of all that he had done and particularly of his father's arrest. His plans for an expedition to quell the rebellious islanders went ahead as the Duke of Lennox was made Lieutenant over the Isles.

Meanwhile the King had decided to make a visit to the Isles in person but was thwarted by various delays. The naval expedition, now commanded by the Duke of Lennox, designed to subdue the rebellious factions in the Isles, was still lying at Dumbarton when Sir Lachlan MacLean of Duart, aware of the falling out between Sir James of Dunyveg and his father and of the former's being at the court in Edinburgh, decided to force the issue over possession of the Rinns of Islay. Sailing from Mull, his galleys crammed with armed men, he approached the head of

Lochgruinart, the wide sea loch penetrating into the north-west of Islay, which all but divided the island from the peninsula of the Rinns.

But Sir James MacDonald had got wind of what was happening. Leaving Edinburgh, he rode across Scotland at a furious speed, taking ship somewhere in either Knapdale or Kintyre, to reach Islay in time to have all his serviceable men in arms before MacLean's galleys were sited bearing down through the Firth of Lorn, from the north.

Sir James was ready for them when they landed. First he made his vanguard take a detour, as if beginning a retreat, but in reality reaching the top of a hill from which he led a deadly charge. The MacLeans fell back in confusion and in the melée Sir Lachlan, a giant of a man easily distinguishable by his height, was fired at by a sharp-shooter, a man from Jura called Shaw, and killed. Sir James himself was badly wounded by an arrow, but his life was saved by one of the Beatons, doctors, or leeches as they then were known, for many generations in Islay.

A year later, in 1599, Sir James MacDonald treated with the King's Comptroller granted by the Privy Council. In the July of the same year, a new commission of Lieutenandry over the whole Isles and Highlands of Inverness-shire was granted to the Duke of Lennox and the Earl of Huntly, by now returned to favour. Then in August the MacDonald chief appeared before the King's Comptroller at Falkland to make certain offers for possession of Kintyre and Islay. He even went so far as to suggest that he take all his clan and dependants out of Kintyre, thus leaving the land entirely at the King's disposal, promising, when new tenants were installed, to 'support and defend them to the utmost of his power.'[69] He also agreed that the castle of Dunyveg, the fortress named by Somerled, conqueror of the Vikings in the 12th century, who beached his nyvegs, or little galleys, below the rocky headland, on the south coast of Islay, should be placed in the hands of a governor and garrison appointed by the King and that sixty merk lands in its vicinity should be assigned for the garrison's maintenance. In return for this, Sir James asked that the rest of Islay, amounting to three hundred merk lands, should be granted to him in heritage for the annual feu-duty of £2 for every merk-land, amounting to £600 in all. In addition he offered to pay his father a yearly pension of one thousand merks, or about £670. Finally, he promised to send his brother, Angus Og, as a hostage for keeping his word and furthermore to pay for his upkeep during his captivity. These suggestions, submitted by the comptroller, were authorised by the Privy Council. However, tragically, as far as Sir James was concerned, for reasons undisclosed, nothing was finalised before King James departed for England.

All the existing evidence suggests that it was the Earl of Argyll, in collaboration with the son who had succeeded the murdered Campbell of Calder, who contrived to prevent the arrangements made between Sir James MacDonald of Dunyveg and the Privy Council from being satisfactorily concluded. Archibald Campbell, 7th Earl of Argyll was known as 'Gillesbuig Grumach' (Archibald the Grim) for good reason. The young man, who having survived an attempt to poison him and had then been defeated at Glenlivet, was now both a seasoned statesman and military commander. Intent on acquiring the lands of Kintyre, he took the part of old Angus, MacDonald, Sir James' father, against his son. Meanwhile, Calder, with his eyes on possessing Islay–although brother-in-law to Sir James MacDonald–incited him to acts of violence which ultimately led to his ruin.

The next to fall foul of Argyll was Alasdair MacGregor of Glenstrae. In 1601, at a meeting of the Privy Council, the King appointed Archibald Earl of Argyll as his lieutenant, with the power to summon the Clan Gregor before him under pain of horning and take sureties of them. If any of them failed to appear he was to 'prosecute them as fugitives and outlaws with fire and sword, to burn their houses and to follow and pursue them wherever they may flee…and to raise fire and use all force and engine which can be had for their capture.' He also had authority to summon their landlords and to hold justice-courts to try them. Anyone who reset a MacGregor, or his wife and children was to be considered guilty of all the bygone or future offences of the clan. Finally, in a deadly promise of his power, the Crown was to have no authority to over-ride Argyll's decisions or to grant mercy to any that he might condemn.[70]

The commission was made retrospective giving power to Argyll to redress all complaints made against the Clan Gregor since 1596. He held his first justice-court at Stirling where

Alasdair MacGregor again undertook obligations to which he had sworn before the Privy Council. He signed the agreement, 'with my hand touching the notary's pen underwritten, because I cannot write.' [71] Alasdair himself, then agreed to remain Argyll's prisoner until he recompensed any individual, either robbed or injured by one of his clan.

Sir Duncan Campbell of Glenorchy was the first to seize advantage of the recent authority given to Argyll. In fairness, he had reason for doing so. Prince Henry, the Prince of Wales, had just given him a much-prized stallion which was grazing on the meadowland around Kilchurn Castle, at the foot of Loch Awe, together with forty mares. A party of MacGregors, hot-headed with resentment, made a night raid and killed the stallion together with many of the mares. It was a cruel and thoughtless deed which played into Sir Duncan's hands giving him the excuse that he needed to raid and destroy Glenstrae. Many of the MacGregors who lived there had their houses burnt and their cattle stolen or killed. Desperately they resisted and many, it seems, died. In 1988, when the floor of Glenorchy Parish Church was lifted during repairs, a mass grave was discovered, the skeletons of men, women and children, packed neatly in rows. Radio-carbon testing proved most of the bones to date from the early 1600s, although the possibility that some of them died from illness, such as the plague, cannot be entirely ruled out.

Argyll then saw a way to make use of Alasdair in his own long-running feud with the Colquhouns of Luss on Loch Lomondside and now luck played on his side. Two MacGregors, returning from Glasgow Fair, were refused shelter for the night by a tenant of the Colquhouns, in the tradition of Highland hospitality, an unforgiveable affront. Much offended, they found an empty barn where they helped themselves to a wedder, (a castrated male sheep) which they killed and ate. Unfortunately, being a black sheep with a white tail, it was quickly missed, and the two marauding MacGregors were quickly caught and hanged. Their murder had to be avenged.

Archibald Grumach was quick to encourage it. "He movit my brother and some of my friends, to commit baith hership and slaughter upon the laird of Luss," Alasdair quoted as saying this, added that, "and when I did refuse his desire in that point, he enticit me with other messengers…to weir and troiuble the laird of Luss, whilk I behovit to do for his false boutgaits."[72]

On the 4 June 1602, Alasdair called out his men for a raid on Luss. With him, went his brother Ian, and his cousins together with about 120 of their men. Down into Glenmulchen they went to lift a whole herd of about 120 cattle, which they successfully drove back, most probably onto the Moor of Rannoch, if not into Glen Strae. Sir Alexander Colquhoun held the Earl of Argyll responsible, under the Royal Commission, for the Clan Gregor's crimes, but Argyll ignored the summons of the Privy Council, thus making the MacGregors believe themselves to be beyond the reach of the law. Subsequently, in early December, one Duncan MacEwin MacGregor, it is thought without Alasdair's permission, made a far more disastrous raid on Glenfinlas, taking everything that moved. No less than 300 cows, 400 sheep and goats and 100 horses were rounded-up and driven away while every cottage was pillaged, the pots and pans and precious lengths of hand-woven cloth seized and carried off. Two of the Colquhouns were killed and many others wounded, struggling to save all they possessed.

The laird, Alexander Colquhoun, went to Dumbarton Castle to try to enlist government aid to punish the men who had done such terrible harm to his people. It was Thomas of Fallasdale, one of the burgesses, who suggested that he should appeal to the King personally, in lieu of the Privy Council, who had done nothing to curb the ravages of the MacGregors. The King was known to be at Stirling so thither Colquhoun went, taking with him the women, wives, mothers and daughters of those who had died or been hurt in Glenfinlas. Riding on horseback, each woman carried her 'bluidy sark' the blood-stained shirt on the end of a spear as she came before the King James' eyes.

The effect was what was expected. James hated and indeed was terrified at the sight of blood. Furious and horrified, he at once issued a commission to Colquhoun, giving him licence to proceed against the Clan Gregor with fire and sword.

Colquhoun acted at once. Rallying his own clan, he enlisted the help of his wife's people, the Buchanans, on the east side of Loch Lomond and beyond. On 8 January 1693, the fencible men were called out while the bailies of Dunbarton saw to their being armed with hackbuts and 'jack, spear and steel-bonnet.' With at least 300 men behind him Colquhoun felt justly confident of wrecking his revenge on the men who had left his own without food, and in many cases even shelter, in the teeth of the winter storms.

Alasdair MacGregor, hearing through the grapevine of how the Colquhouns were mustering against him, summoned his own men to arms. From Rannoch, he crossed the hills to Balquhidder, following the line of the old drove road, which has become the A 85 today. Together with his men he slept, wrapped in his plaid, wherever he could find shelter, on a barn or the lee of a dyke, or if needs must on the bare ground hard with frost. After Tyndrum, or Clifton as it then was known, he would have turned east at Crianlarich and from there through Glen Dochart, below the towering Ben More, before turning south up Glen Ogle to come down to Lochearnhead. From thence, after some miles, it was a short turn off to Balquhidder at the foot of Loch Voil.

There Alasdair was joined by his brother Ian, who had rallied a large body of MacGregors together with some men from other clans. From Balquhidder they crossed the hills, probably through Glen Arklet, to reach the head of Loch Lomond, from where they would have pursued their way through the narrow isthmus of Tarbert to Loch Long. From Garelochhead they reached the top of Glen Fruin the Highlanders, used to such country, making little of the steepness of the climb. Then, descending to the boggy ground at the mouth of the glen, Alasdair made his stand.

Colquhoun's cavalry were useless, floundering in the mud. Seeing this happen, the MacGregors charged, screaming their battle cry of Ard Choile. Alasdair's brother fell dead, shot by an arrow, but his men pursued the enemy, sending Colquhoun's foot soldiers fleeing in confusion down the glen. Soon the retreat became a massacre as the MacGregors pursued. In all it is estimated that 120 of the Colquhouns were slain, including some of the burgesses of Dumbarton. Alexander Colquhoun, himself, his horse killed under him, only just made it to safety to his castle of Rossdhu.

Then, inevitably, elated by their triumph, Alasdair's men raided the whole district, carrying off an estimated 600 cattle, in addition to many horses and sheep, burning and pillaging as they went.

CHAPTER 22
The Man with a Pot of Gold

Another who joined James' enemies was a young man of twenty-three, who recently returned from the Continent, offered to serve Queen Elizabeth, at that time in verbal if not military contest with her cousin, the Scottish King.

This was John Ruthven, 3rd Earl of Gowrie, born c. 1577, who, as the younger son of the 1st Earl, had succeeded, his elder brother, the 2nd Earl, in 1586. John Ruthven had followed the family tradition of adhering to the Protestant faith, allying himself to the most strident reformers. In 1592, when only fifteen, he had contrived his election to his family's customary position of Provost of Perth. Notably clever as a boy, he had received a good education, first, at Perth Grammar School and then at Edinburgh University, at which latter place he was attending when his mother and his sister helped Bothwell to enter Holyrood Palace.

Thereafter, while almost certainly involved with Bothwell in his plans to either kidnap or kill King James, he thought it expedient, in 1594, to leave Scotland and go to Italy, with his tutor, William Rhynd to study at the University of Padua. Returning after five years, he stayed for some time in Geneva where the reformer, Theodore Beza, inspired him with his radical ideas.

Reaching Paris, he got to know the English ambassador, Henry Neville, who, writing to Queen Elizabeth's secretary Robert Cecil, on 27 February 1599, told him that Guthrie was devoted to his sovereign's cause. He would like, so Neville told Cecil, to kiss the Queen's hand and if granted this honour could give her some valuable information regarding the political state of Scotland which, under the King's auspices, had been undergoing reforms. Given this information Queen Elizabeth received him graciously, as did her ministers, when, after leaving Paris, he reached the English court. So well was he welcomed that it was not until May 1600 that Gowrie reached Scotland after being away for eight years.

Now aged about twenty-two, he had been at home for three months, when, on 5 August 1600, he became involved in the conspiracy, which, despite the best efforts of historians throughout the centuries, has never been satisfactorily solved. So many theories have been put forward that the King's own version of the extraordinary events of that day, may after all, be the one closest to the truth.

James declared that, on the morning of that fateful 5 August at Falkland Palace, he had risen early to go hunting when, at the gate of the castle 'the young Master of Ruthven (Alexander, younger brother of the earl), his eyes fixed strangely upon the ground, had drawn him aside and whispering that he had found a stranger in Perth carrying a pot of gold, had begged him to come and investigate.'

The King, according to his own version, had at first refused, but Alexander's story kept running in his mind. The Ruthvens had bated their trap well, aware, as were most people in the court, of their monarch's desperate shortage of money. Tempted beyond endurance, he later in the day turned his horse's head and rode to Perth, a distance of some fourteen miles, accompanied by only sixteen attendants, all very lightly armed.

Arriving, John Gowrie seemed surprised to see him, to the point where the King had to wait for an hour before a scratch meal of some sort was produced. Then, having eaten, he was taken by Gowrie's younger brother, Alexander, the Master of Ruthven, up the main staircase and through two rooms and two doors, both of which Alexander locked behind him, into a turret-room at the angle of the house which overlooked both the courtyard and the street.

This was where James expected to find the mysterious stranger with the pot of gold. Instead, he found himself faced with an armed man, who turned out to be a servant of Gowrie's called Henderson. At that moment Alexander Ruthven suddenly put on his hat and drawing his servant's dagger out of his belt, held it to the King's throat, swearing to cut it immediately if James dared to call for help.

Blaming him for the death of his father, Alexander held the blade before the King's eyes. But James, despite his terror contriving to stay calm, managed to prolong his life by pointing out the many benefits, which during successive years, the Ruthven family had received from the crown. Alexander, apparently convinced, then removed his hat, and telling James that his life would be safe if he did not cry for help, left him in the care of the servant Henderson, while he went to consult with his brother, locking the door behind him as he went.

Lord Gowrie, in the meantime, had told those in the rooms below that the King, having mounted his horse, had ridden away. Fortunately for James, however, his own followers, perhaps suspicious of what was happening, had stayed within earshot of Gowrie House.

Meanwhile, on Alexander's departure, King James had begun questioning the servant, Henderson, as to what plot, if any, was afoot. On Henderson proving evasive, about something of which he probably did not know the answer, James complained, that it being the month of August, the small room in the turret was excessively hot. Henderson, eager to please him, opened one of the two windows and was about to open the other when Alexander Ruthven returned.

Seeing James standing by the window, he began to try to bind his hands, but James, finding unknown strength in his terror, struggling to resist him, managed to edge towards the open window. Shouting, "treason!" He yelled for the Earl of Mar. Gowrie pretended not to hear anything but Mar and most of those with him ran up the main staircase to help the King.

Met by the locked door they spent some time battering it down, but, while they were doing this, John Ramsay (later the Earl of Holderness) espied a dark stairway running up to the small inner chamber adjoining the turret. Up it he pounded, again to meet a locked door. But Henderson, by now badly frightened, unlocked it on his urgent demand. Bursting into the room, Ramsay found the King struggling with Alexander Ruthven, and drawing his dagger, he wounded Ruthven before pushing him down the stairway past the King. Thomas Erskine, Mar's brother, and Doctor Hugh Herries, their swords drawn, then came dashing up the stair to fall on Alexander and kill him.

Alexander's brother, John Earl of Gowrie, at that moment crossing the courtyard with his stabler, Thomas Cranstoun, seeing Alexander's body lying motionless and bleeding in the stairwell, pushed past it to rush upwards and in the short, desperate fight that followed, he himself was killed.

The news of what had happened on that momentous afternoon at Guthrie House tore through Scotland and down into England with the force of a rip tide. The ministers of the Kirk, only with great scepticism, accepted the King's version of what had occurred. They believed that James had invented his story to cover his determination to exterminate the Ruthven family to whom he was greatly in debt. The 1st Earl of Ruthven, while treasurer, had lent no less than £48,063 to cover the expenses of the government in the early years of James' reign. This sum, with the annual interest of 10%, had amounted to £80,000 over the intervening years. It was probably because of his penury that John, the young earl, had gone to live abroad. Returning, on 20 June 1600, he had successfully obtained protection from debt for the period of a year.

On 7 August 1600, the Privy Council directed that the corpses of the Earl of Gowrie and his brother Alexander Ruthven, must remain unburied and that no one with the name of Ruthven should approach within ten miles of the court. The bodies of Gowrie and his brother were eventually disembowelled and on 30 October were sent to Edinburgh to be produced at the bar of Parliament before being hanged and quartered at the Mercat Cross. The heads were then put on spikes at the Old Tolbooth and the arms and legs distributed to various locations around the Ruthven's home town of Perth. On 15 November the estates of the family were forfeited to the crown and their family name and honours declared to be extinct. Then, by a separate Act of Parliament, the house where the murders had happened was ordered to be levelled to the ground, while the barony of Ruthven was henceforth to be known as that of Huntingtower.[73]

William and Patrick Ruthven, Gowrie's two younger surviving brothers, managed to escape to England. William is believed to have reached Virginia where he changed his name to Ruffin, while Patrick was less fortunate, being taken prisoner and held in the Tower of London for no less than nineteen years.

So what was the real reason for what is known to this day as the Gowrie Conspiracy? Was it in fact a plan of the Gowrie brothers to capture the King? Or was it really cupidity on the part of the latter to escape from overwhelming debt? Today the only thing that seems certain, is that that we shall never know.

CHAPTER 23
Diplomacy and Retribution

Yet, despite the allegations delivered against him of personal cupidity being the cause for the destruction of the family of Ruthven, King James, by the end of the first year of the new century beginning with 1600, was now more than ever controller of his country.

In the towns and cities in the greater part of Scotland trade was improving, while the standard of living of most people, although not comparable with England, was certainly higher than in any of the reigns of the King's immediate predecessors. Possessed, as he would seem to have been, of an inborn understanding of human nature, James was quick to understand that the rising importance of the burgesses, forming a middle class, was an antidote to the hitherto largely unchallenged power of the nobles and the Presbyterian Kirk.

It was now forty years since Presbyterianism had been established by the Parliament of 1560 as the recognised Scottish creed. Nevertheless the King's predominance was so strong that in July 1600, when he had brought forward the idea that bishops be nominated as representatives of the church in Parliament, he was able to nominate three bishops himself. Although decried by Andrew Melville, the great Scottish Reformer and uncle of Sir James, as 'God's silly vassal' James VI of Scotland, now King for thirty-three years, had proved himself to be not only a born politician but a shrewd manipulator of men who through sheer common-sense; had contrived to make the warring factions of religion support both his rule in Scotland and his prospects of becoming England's King.

It was during his last years in Scotland that James became an author.

Obsessed as he was with witchcraft and the existence of the Devil, in whom he implicitly believed, he explained his ideas on the subject in a book entitled *Daemonologie* by King James VI of Scotland. Written in the form of a dialogue, it is divided into three books, which, while originally printed in Edinburgh in 1597, are now held in the Bodleian Library in Oxford.

James began with a preface, explaining that it was:

"The fearefull aboundings at this time in the countrie, of these detestable slaves of the Devill, the witches or enchanters, hath moved me (beloved reader) to dispatch in post this following treatie of mine."

The First Book contained what the King described as:

"An Argument Proven by the Scripture that these unlawful artes of this sort (in genre) have bene and may be put in practise."

The Second Book, again in the form of an argument is headed, 'The description of Sorcerie and witch-craft in Special.'

The Third, 'The description of these kindes of Spirites that troubles men or women,' is followed by the conclusion of the whole dialogue.

Published later in England, in 1603, the book explains James' fascination, amounting almost to an obsession, with the powers of evil, embodied within individuals either with or without their conscious assent.

Once inspired by authorship, the King could not lay down his pen.

Hardly a year had passed before a treatise, headed *The Trew Law of Free Monarchies: or the Reciprock and Mutuall Dutie Berwixt a Free King and his Naturall Subjects*, was published in September 1598. Basing his work on the Scriptures he explained the Divine Right of kings, as having been begun by God's own ordinance:

'The warning that God gave to Samuel, that a king would bring many burdens, was to prepare the people's hearts for the obedience they must yield to a king, who they must obey and retain forever. It has been argued that men should remove a tyrannical king. But evil kings as well as good ones come from God, and men may not remove the curse that God has placed upon them.'

This volume was followed by the *Basilikon Doron*, written in three parts, primarily for the edification of Prince Henry, then a little boy of four years. James, convinced apparently of his own early demise, laid down precise instructions for the son who would succeed him as King. Prince Henry was told emphatically that he must 'possess every virtue, eschew every vice, and stand before his people as a model of self-restraint, wisdom and godliness.' Privately and secretly printed in 1599, there were only seven copies, which the King gave to his most trusted friends. Then later, reprinted and on sale in London, it became a best-seller, bought by ambassadors to send to their governments and eventually translated into most of the European languages. King James 'the wisest fool in Christendom,' as later Sir Anthony Weldon would disrespectfully call him, was respected as an oracle of his day.

The King was now ruling Scotland most efficiently through his Council. Always a conciliator, to the point where he was criticised for being too lenient with offenders, he had succeeded in establishing some pacification between the warring religious parties and in 1599, is believed have even signed a propitiatory letter to the Pope.[74]

He was also in secret correspondence with the Earl of Essex, Queen Elizabeth's brilliant but unstable favourite, whose struggle for ultimate power with her Secretary of State, Robert Cecil, resulted in civil war. Early in 1599 Essex was sent to Ireland with 17,000 soldiers to try to overcome the rebellious Earl of Tyrone who, on 14 August of the previous year of 1598, had annihilated an English army at the battle of the Yellow Ford on the Blackwater River.

Acting on Queen Elizabeth's orders, and after some failed operations in the south of the country, Essex had met Tyrone at a ford on the River Lagan, where, on 7 September 1599, he had arranged a truce with Tyrone ceding largely to the Irish lord's demands interpreted in England as being most reprehensible terms. Queen Elizabeth, when told, retorted sharply that if she had intended to abandon Ireland she would not have sent Essex there in the first place!

Later, two of his followers would confess that Essex had tried to get the King of Scots to help him during his Irish campaign and it appears that a plan had been suggested, by which James would lead an army to the Borders and there announce his right to be King of England following Queen Elizabeth's demise.

James did eventually despatch the Earl of Mar to deal with Essex but Mar arrived in London only to find that Essex himself was dead. Goaded by a passionate loathing of his enemies, he had tried to raise a force of his supporters in London with whom he intended to force entry to Queen Elizabeth and to summon a Parliament that would recognise James as her successor. The attempt had failed and Essex, arrested in his own house on 9 February 1601, had been tried and executed within the space of three weeks.

Mar was coldly treated in London until suddenly a coup d'état took place. Summoned to a secret interview he was told by Cecil, that subject to stringent strictures, he would correspond with King James to promote his interests in England.

There followed an extraordinary correspondence between James and Queen Elizabeth's First Minister using a secret code. Cecil himself was 10, Queen Elizabeth 24, the Earl of Northumberland 0 and James 30. 'My dearest and trusty Cecil,' wrote the King, 'my pen is not able to express how happy I think myself for having chanced upon, so worthy, so wise, so provident a friend.'

The exchange of letters, beginning in 1601 and continuing for two years, resulted in Cecil's increasing influence over James, who eventually described him as 'his dearest and most truest 10.'[75] Cecil told him how to flatter Queen Elizabeth, whom he now addressed as his, 'richt excellent, richt heich and michtie princesse, our dearest sister and cousine,' to whom the Queen replied in a similar way, calling him her, 'dear brother."

Many men in both England and Scotland, precipitating James's accession to Elizabeth's throne, had to be misinformed as to what was so clandestinely taking place. To the Master of Gray, trying to climb on the bandwagon, Cecil even pretended a violent hostility between himself and the King of Scots. But Cecil, alert to what was taking place, told James 'to be steadfast,' assuring him that, on the now expected death of Queen Elizabeth, people in England would come to regard him as her rightful successor.

The inevitable happened when, on 24 March 1603, Queen Elizabeth died. Sir Robert Carey, who had horses posted all the way up the North road, rode almost non-stop to Edinburgh to be first to take the news to James. On 5 April the new King of Great

Britain, as he proudly named himself, set out on his journey to London, capital city of the country over which, in his own estimation, he knew he had been born to rule.

CHAPTER 24
The Arrow of Glenlyon

But what was to happen to the Scots whom he left behind?

Queen Elizabeth was dead. King James, accepted as her successor, was just about to depart for England. Nonetheless, only two days before leaving, he found time to summon the Scottish Council to deal with the Clan MacGregor. The name itself was proscribed, to use it meant punishment with death. Alasdair, the chief, the 'Arrow of Glenlyon' to his people, and all those who had taken part in the battle in Glen Fruin were declared outlaws and a price put on the heads of all the clan. Anyone who killed a MacGregor would be rewarded with all that he owned and, in the case of his being outlawed himself, would receive a pardon. In Argyll Sir Duncan Campbell of Glenorchy kept bloodhounds to hound down any MacGregors who dared to linger on what, for so many centuries, had been their land.

Much of the spoils from Glen Fruin had gone to Campbell of Ardkinlas Alasdair, calling Ardkinlas, 'the man I did maist trust unto,' went, it is thought alone, to his castle at the head of Loch Fyne. He believed that his friend would protect him, but Ardkinlas, terrified of the Earl of Argyll, his overlord as well as his chief, instead took him prisoner in an act of betrayal that sickened his very heart.

On 2 October, with his hands bound behind him, Alasdair was forced into a boat to be taken down Loch Fyne to Argyll's castle of Inveraray at the mouth of the Aray Glen. With him went five guards, all of them strong men. It seemed that his fate was certain. But somehow, with the superhuman strength born of desperation, he managed to free his hands, to strike down the man next to him and leap overboard. Swimming and diving to avoid the bullets the other guards fired over his head, he succeeded in reaching the shore.

From there he contrived to vanish, probably on the Moor of Rannoch where he knew every hiding place and where his own men would warn him of enemies approaching from afar. Wherever it was that he hid, a message managed to reach him from the Earl of Argyll. He was innocent of Ardkinlas' treachery, so he claimed. It had been entirely his own idea. Alasdair would make his peace with the King and gain his pardon if only he would surrender himself without any show of arms. Argyll promised that he would then send him over the border into England from where he could go to find King James.

Alasdair had won the King's pardon before in those days when he had resided at the court. Seeing himself with little or no alternative, he decided to take Argyll at his word. Argyll did as he had promised, sending Alasdair as far as Berwick escorted by an armed guard. But once over the border he was immediately seized by a company of the town guard of Edinburgh who carried him back to their city as a prisoner.

It was late in the January of 1604 that the MacGregor chief was brought up for what proved to a mock trial. The jury included burgesses of Dumbarton whose relatives had been killed in the battle of Glenfruin, who naturally showed no mercy for the man they held responsible for their slaughter. Accused on the capital charge of high treason he was hanged the next day at the Mercat Cross in Edinburgh. The only privilege allowed to him, that of being suspended at his own height above several of his clan in token of his rank. His head, sent to Dumbarton, was fixed above the town tollbooth so that the people of that town could feel themselves avenged.

Three years later, as reward for his loyal services against Clan Gregor, the King gave the lands of Kintyre to Archibald Grumach, 7th Earl of Argyll [76]

PART 2

CHAPTER 1
King James I of Great Britain

On 5 April 1603, King James left Edinburgh to begin his ride to London. Reaching Berwick, attended by some of the great border chiefs, he was presented with a purse of gold as canons roared out in welcome making the earth tremble and filling the town with smoke. Leaving Berwick, he proved his fitness by riding forty miles in four hours, his retinue struggling to keep up with him on horses lathered with sweat. At York he met Robert Cecil, the little hunch-backed lawyer, who had been such a bulwark of Elizabeth's regime. James immediately asked him for money—he had spent all he had by the time of reaching Berwick—and for jewels and ladies-in-waiting for Queen Anne. Avaricious as he probably thought this to be, Cecil was none the less impressed with James, writing that 'I have made so sufficient a discovery of his royal perfections, as I contemplate greater felicity to this isle than it ever enjoyed.'[77]

Meanwhile the King had continued riding south to Doncaster and from thence on to Worksop and Belvoir Castle in Rutland to be magnificently entertained by the Earls of Shrewsbury and Rutland. Hares, brought in baskets, were let loose to be hunted by hounds. Reaching Burghley House, the seat of Cecil's older brother, inheritor of their father's title, James unfortunately fell off his horse and broke his collar-bone, after which he had to travel by coach.

This was disappointing for the multitude of people who had flocked in from the locality to see their new King ride by. Reaching Cecil's own house called Theobolds, some twelve miles north of London, James was met by the Lord Mayor and Aldermen, with five hundred citizens, all well mounted and clad in velvet cloaks emblazoned with golden chains. The press was soon almost unbearable to the point where, as one observer wrote, 'the multitude of people on highways, fields, meadows, and on trees were such that they covered the beauty of the fields,' and so greedy were they to behold the countenance of the King that, with much unruliness, they injured and hurt one another, following the King with shouts and cries and casting up of hats.

Finally, to escape the crowds, James made his way to the Charterhouse through outlying fields to reach Aldergate, to board a barge that carried him up the Thames to the Tower of London.

From the Tower he explored his new capital city, before, in the ensuing months, visiting the royal houses that lay within the home counties, where, to his great delight, he found deer and other game in the surrounding parks for hunting 'which is the sport he preferreth above all worldly delights and pastimes.'

His hunting, at that time, when still in the prime of life, was a very dangerous form of sport. Running hounds were set on the scent of a stag and the riders followed at a wild gallop over the surrounding country. When the hounds killed the King was the first to dismount and, extraordinary as it was for a man known to detest the sight of blood, cut the stag's throat and slit open its belly into which he plunged his hands and sometimes even his feet. He then daubed the faces of the courtiers, who had managed to keep up with him, with blood as a sign of his great esteem. [78]

The arrival of Queen Anne from Scotland then caused even greater excitement. Lady Anne Clifford, daughter of the Earl of Cumberland, described how she and her mother killed three horses by over-driving them in their haste to meet the Queen and that when she joined James at Windsor 'there was such an infinite number of lords and ladies and so great a court as I think I shall never see the like again.'[79] Also, rather charmingly, she relates how the King was overjoyed to see his children. In jovial and homely fashion he turned to a courtier asking him, in his broad, Scot's accent, did he not think his Annie looked passing well? Then, lifting up the seven-year-old Elizabeth and kissing her, 'my little Bessy too, is not an ill-faured wench and may outshine her mother one of these days.' A great banquet then took place at Windsor, the highlight of which being Prince Henry's investment with the Order of the Garter.

Anne charmed everyone upon her entry into London. 'Our gracious Queen, mild and courteous, placed in a chariot of exceeding beauty, did all the way so humbly and with mildness salute her subjects, never leaving to bend her body this way and that, that men and women wept for joy.'

King James himself, also made a good impression as described by the Venetian ambassador who, when given his first audience at Greenwich, soon after his arrival in England in May 1603, had to fight through the crowds to reach him.

"I found all the Council around his chair, and an infinity of other lords almost in an attitude of adoration. His Majesty rose and took six steps towards the middle of the room [and] he then remained standing while he listened to me attentively. He was dressed in grey silver satin, quite plain with a cloak of black tabbinet reaching below his knees and lined with crimson, he had his arm in a white sling, the result of a fall from his horse; from his dress he would have been taken as the meanest among his courtiers, a modesty he affects, had it not been for a chain of diamonds around his neck and a great diamond in his hat.'

'The King's countenance is handsome, noble and jovial,' wrote an Italian at the court, 'his colour blond, his hair somewhat the same, his beard square and lengthy, his mouth small, his eyes blue, his nose curved and clear-cut, a man happily formed, neither fat nor thin, of full vitality, neither too large nor too small.'

It was fortunate, that through their secret correspondence, James had established such a good relationship with Robert Cecil. Both their interchange of letters and the reports of ambassadors to Scotland, had primed Cecil for what to expect.

But if Cecil was ready for James most of Elizabeth's erstwhile servitors were not. Many were amazed, and in some cases horrified by the familiarity of this new monarch forced upon them by right of birth by his relationship from their venerated Queen. To them this Scotsman of thirty-seven, who, thanks to the deformation of his right foot, walked in a shambling way, his arms on other men's shoulders to support his weight, was a savage from a foreign land who talked, or rather spluttered volubly in the barely decipherable, broad Scots' tongue.

Nonetheless, uncouth as he appeared to be, he was at least approachable. The stiff etiquette of Elizabeth's court was to some extent relaxed. Queen Anne was found to be charming and gracious, as was the nine–year-old Prince Henry, the Prince of

Wales. His sister Princess Elizabeth, in particular, two years younger than Henry, was already showing signs of the beauty for which she would later be famed. The two youngest children, the three-year-old Prince Charles, small for his age and shy and the two-year-old Princess Mary, being of less significance than their older siblings, possessed as they were of such striking and obvious good looks.

King James arrived in England to find himself faced with worse and more divisive religious problems than he had met in Scotland, while adhering to the Presbyterian creed, he had favoured Episcopalians, seeing bishops as the natural supporters of the crown. But in England there were more Catholics, their influence an ever present threat to the Protestant Church of England as established by Henry VIII and adhered to by his daughter Queen Elizabeth.

It was largely due to Cecil, with whom through their secret correspondence he had established a rapport, that James was accepted as monarch by the English government over which Cecil, as first minister, held sway. Robert Cecil, the younger son of Elizabeth's great secretary Lord Burleigh by his second wife Mildred Cooke, was remarkable both for the smallness of his size and from an early age the brilliance of his mind. Born in 1563, both undersized and a hunchback, he was cruelly ridiculed at a time when physical strength was considered essential to a man. Queen Elizabeth called him 'my pygmy' and James 'my little beagle.' Yet despite his physical disabilities his father was quick to recognise that it was Robert, rather than his older half-brother Thomas, who had inherited his own brilliant mind. 'Robert could rule England,' he said, 'but Thomas could hardly rule a tennis court.'

Robert Cecil had been educated both at St John's College Cambridge and at the Sorbonne before, most importantly, he was instructed to be a spymaster by Sir Francis Walsingham, Queen Elizabeth's famous expert in the art of subterfuge. While already a Privy Councillor in his father's government, on the latter's death in 1598, he had stepped into the great man's shoes. His rivalry with the Queen's other favourite, the Earl of Essex, which resulted in the rebellion, aimed at Cecil's death, had ended with Essex's execution in 1601. It was Cecil who had persuaded the Queen to pardon the majority of the rebels, but nonetheless, at the time of James' arrival in London, Cecil was vilified in public, lampooned as a villain unhung. Despite this, regardless of popular feeling, the new king, who in their exchange of missives had recognised Cecil's integrity and outstanding ability, raised him to the peerage as Lord Cecil of Essendon before making him Viscount Cranbourne in the following year and eventually Earl of Salisbury in 1605.

Cecil's loyalty to the new monarch was tested soon after James' arrival in London when the King's life was threatened by two treacherous schemes, known as the Bye Plot and the Main Plot in which Cecil's own brother-in-law, Lord Cobham was involved. These were attempts by ardent Catholics, to either kill or kidnap James and put Lady Arbella Stuart, the twenty-eight-year-old daughter of the now deceased Charles, Earl of Lennox (younger brother of James' father, Henry Lord Darnley) on the throne. Arbella herself a slim, rather delicate young woman with ash blond hair, kept under close surveillance by her maternal grandmother, the formidable Bess of Hardwick, knew nothing of what was happening, or being planned in her name.

First to take action were two Roman Catholic priests, William Watson and William Clark, who, together with a Protestant George Brooke, plotted to kidnap the King and hold him in the Tower of London until he agreed to end the persecution of English Catholics. This, the Bye Plot, was leaked to Robert Cecil, who showed no mercy to the two priests who were executed, brutally hung drawn and quartered in a way to cause the maximum of pain.

More serious was the Main Plot which involved no less a person than Sir Walter Raleigh, who, together with Lord Cobham (brother of George Brooke as well as brother-in-law of Cecil), Lord Grey de Wilton and Griffin Markham, the latter a Roman Catholic friend of the family of Arabella Stuart, schemed to replace James on the throne. An appeal to Henry IV of France for financial assistance was peremptorily refused before, in July 1603, all those in both plots were arrested, and in November, brought to trial.

George Brooke was executed, but the King, anxious not to antagonise his subjects of the Catholic faith, ordered the reprieve of Cobham, Grey de Wilton and Griffin Markham while they were literally at the scaffold steps. Raleigh, described as, 'the most hated man in England,'[80]due to be hanged a few days later, was then also pardoned by the magnanimous King, thanks largely, it was believed, to Cecil's mitigation on his behalf.

CHAPTER 2
Gunpowder, Treason and Plot

King James' absorption in religion, in common with so many of his time, had already been made manifest when, while still in Scotland in 1601, in an eloquent speech to the General Assembly of the Kirk, he had urged the translation of the Geneva Bible into words which most citizens could understand. Now, in England, in 1604, translators had been found. James himself had overseen the choice and given detailed instructions for them to follow. No less than fifty-four translators were divided into six groups, in London, Oxford and Cambridge by men who were professors of Hebrew.

James ordered that the Bishop's Bible be followed as far as possible, that proper names, already familiar to the people should be used, and that notes in the margins should be omitted except to explain the double use of words. The King was determined that his new Bible should be written in a way that ordinary people could easily understand.

It was as he was riding through England on his journey from Scotland in the spring of 1603, that the new King of England had been forced to diverge from his hunting to receive a delegation from the Puritan clergy who presented him with the ultimately famous Millenary Petition. Its authors insisted that they trusted to the Christian judgement of their dread sovereign to lighten their burdens, protesting that they were not factious men like the Scottish Presbyterians, but loyal subjects of the King. The latter part of the statement was misleading. James was only later to discover that the two forms of religion were virtually allied.

In fact he was more tolerant of the English Roman Catholics than he was of the Puritans. Before even leaving Scotland he had written to Cecil that he would 'seek a golden mean' in dealing with English Roman Catholics, his one over-riding desire being that Catholics and Protestants would unite in one faith.

On 19 March 1604, the King attended his first English Parliament. In a speech he proclaimed his great determination to secure peace but 'only by profession of the true religion.' Reiterating his wish to achieve a Christian union, however, he then made it clear to the Catholics that 'they were not to increase their number and strength in the Kingdom, that they might be in hope to erect their Religion again.'

For the Catholics this meant renewed persecution and their fears were confirmed when, on 24 April, a bill was passed in Parliament to outlaw all English followers of the Catholic Church.

The intrigues began again. The main aim of the insurgents was to kill the King but they also connived to kidnap his daughter, Princess Elizabeth, the third in the line of succession, who was then living at Coombe Abbey, near Coventry, conveniently close to the Midlands' stronghold of the Catholic hierarchy. Once in their hands, with her father dead, they planned to make her the Queen.

Foremost amongst the conspirators was Robert Catesby, a noticeably handsome man in his early thirties. 'His countenance exceedingly noble and expressive,' he was also renowned for his skill as a swordsman. Described as a charismatic and influential man who had an irresistible influence over the minds of those who associated with him. He was a religious zealot, who believed in all sincerity that the innocent must suffer if the true faith were to be restored.

Born in Warwickshire in about 1572, Catesby was educated at Gloucester Hall in Oxford but, his family being well-known recusant Catholics, he left the university, to avoid taking the Oath of Supremacy, (requiring any person taking public or church office in England to swear allegiance to the monarch as Supreme Governor of the Church of England) without taking his degree. Later he may have studied at the Catholic College of Douai. Devoted as he was to the Catholic cause, in 1603 he nonetheless married a Protestant lady, Catherine Leigh, daughter of an Oxfordshire neighbour, who came with a dowry of £2,000, with whom he had two children one of whom survived to be baptised in a Protestant church. However, upon the death of both his wife and his father (himself a martyr to his faith) he is thought to have converted to a form of fanatical Catholicism.

In 1601 Catesby had taken part in the Earl of Essex's rebellion against the government of Queen Elizabeth, a failed rising scornfully described by the Queen herself as both 'perilous and contemptible.' Taken prisoner and heavily fined, he had been forced to sell his estate at Chastleton in Oxfordshire.

Once again, just like Drumquhassle in Scotland, he was the driving force behind a sworn intention, in this case to murder the King. But here the comparison ended. Whereas Drumquhassle, if Melville is to be believed, was entirely out to benefit himself and his friends, Catesby, in the words of the modern historian, Lady Antonia Fraser, 'had the mind of the crusader who does not hesitate to employ the sword in the cause of values which he considers are spiritual.'[81]

Already in the previous year of 1603 Catesby had helped to organise a mission to Philip III, King of Spain with the purpose of persuading him to invade England where, so Catesby had assured him, the Catholics would rise in force to his aid. Thomas Winter, a cousin of Catesby, a fluent linguist and mercenary soldier who had fought in the Spanish Netherlands, was chosen as the emissary to the Spanish King. But Philip, although sympathetic to their cause, was intent on keeping peaceful relations with the new British monarch.

Robert Catesby then was the man who, in in the early part of 1604, was inspired with the idea of destroying both the King and the members of the House of Lords by blowing them up with gunpowder, later to become so famous as the Gunpowder Plot.

The seeds of the scheme seem to have been sown in his mind by his friend Thomas Percy, a great-grandson of the 4th Earl of Northumberland said to have been a 'wild youth' before taking the pledge to become a Catholic. As such he had been sent by his cousin, the 9th Earl of Northumberland, on a secret errand to King James' court in Scotland to try to persuade the King to help the persecuted Catholics in England.[82] It was reported that Thomas Percy had been assured of an accommodation that would allow them to worship discreetly and have their grievances amended. James, who at the time seems to have made some uncompromising reply, would afterwards deny that he had given any promise of Catholic emancipation. Percy, swearing that he had broken his word, on the outbreak of persecution now ranted against what he construed to be James' treachery to the point where he threatened to kill him.

'No, no, Tom, thou shall not venture to small purpose, but if thou wilt be a traitor thou shalt be to some great advantage,' said Catesby interrupting his tirade, 'I am thinking of the most sure way and will soon let thee know what it is.' Then, while Percy waited to be told what his friend intended, Catesby sent for his cousin Thomas Winter who, together with his brother Robert Winter was at Huddington Court in Worcestershire. Thomas, trained as a lawyer, who had also converted to Catholicism, at first refused to come but when Catesby renewed pressure on him, he did appear in the February of that fateful year of 1605.

Thomas Winter, described as, 'a man of mean stature, and rather low, than otherwise, square-made, somewhat stooping, near 40 years of age; his hair and his beard brown, his beard not much, and his hair short,' was also praised by a friend as, 'one of the wisest and most resolute and sufficient gentlemen in Worcestershire.'[83] An intelligent, witty and educated man, he could speak Latin, Italian, Spanish and French. Beginning his career as a lawyer, but inspired by a love of adventure, he had abandoned his profession to travel to Flanders to fight in the British army against Catholic Spain in the Netherlands, in France and possibly even against the Turks in Central Europe.

But then had come his conversion. Inspired by his new faith he had gone to Spain in 1602 to petition the Council on behalf of the Catholics, who had been persecuted since the failure of the Rising of the Earl of Essex. This visit to Spain was followed by another, timed unfortunately after the failure of the Spanish attack on Ireland, which was later to be cited against him as the 'Spanish Treason.'

It was in February 1604 that Robert Catesby, asked his cousin Thomas Winter to come to his house in Lambeth. Thomas replied that this was impossible because he was ill. On receiving a second summons, however, he did obey his cousin's wish.

Once there, he found Robert Catesby with a man renowned as a swordsman called John Wright. Catesby detailed his plan to kill the King, together with his government, by blowing up 'the Parliament house with gunpowder…in that place have they done us all the mischief, and perchance God hath designed that place for their punishment.'[84]

Winter at first prevaricated, appalled, it would seem by the enormity of his cousin's intentions, but Catesby scoffing at his fear, told him that, 'the nature of the disease required so sharp a remedy at which Winter succumbed to the well-known charm of this reputedly captivating man. He did, however, warn him of the backlash of failure, ramming it in that, 'the scandal would be so great which the Catholic religion might hereby sustain, as not only our enemies, but our friends also would withgo reason condemn us,'[85] Then, having issued these dire words, he did agree to join the conspiracy before departing back to Flanders.

It was in one of the French Channel ports, that in April 1604, Thomas Winter had first met Juan Fernández de Velasco, Duke of Frias and Constable of Castile who was just about to depart to finalise the Treaty of London at Somerset House. To him Winter had pleaded most anxiously for the English Catholics, but the Constable had been uncompromising in his reply.

It was on this expedition, however, that Winter also came across Hugh Owen, the Welsh spy, who in turn introduced him to Guy or Guido Fawkes. Although born in Yorkshire of Protestant parents, it seems that it was through the influence of John Pulley, headmaster of St Peter's in York, the school that he attended, that, Guy, had become a Catholic, now as fervent as Winter himself.

The two men had much in common. Both had been mercenary soldiers, Fawkes having sold his inheritance in England to fight for Catholic Spain against the Protestant Dutch Republic and then for a time in France. Subsequently he had joined his fellow Catholic, Sir William Stanley who had conscripted an army in Ireland to fight in the Earl of Leicester's expedition to the Netherlands. But following the surrender of the city of Deventer in the Netherlands to the Spanish, in 1587, Stanley like most of his soldiers, had changed sides to fight for Spain.

Winter went to Ostend to meet his old commander Sir William Stanley and ask him specifically about Fawkes' 'sufficiency in the wars,' Stanley gave 'a very good commendations of him,' thus providing Catesby with a reference for the man whose name, despite the fact that it was originally Catesby's idea, is linked forever with the Gunpowder Plot.

It was in Ostend that Winter explained Catesby's plans, inspiring Fawkes with admiration, both for the courage of the man intending to kill the King for suppressing the Catholic religion, and for the sheer audacity of what he intended to do.

Fawkes, while still a young officer, had fought in the siege of Calais in 1596, his name being put forward for a captaincy by 1603. In that same year, however, forsaking his promising career, he had travelled to Spain to look for support with both money and men to aid a rebellion in England. Under his Spanish name of Guido, he had contrived an audience with King Philip III, who, although receiving him cordially, had then had to listen to a diatribe against both King James, described by Fawkes as a, 'heretic, who intended to have all the papists driven out of England' and his favourites, particularly the Scottish nobles, who he claimed would soon disrupt the realm. He ranted on until King Philip, having listened politely, refused to provide assistance in any practical way.

Together Fawkes and Winter returned to Greenwich, from where, they took 'a two-pair of oars' to row up the Thames to Catesby's house in Lambeth. There, with a group of several others, they continued to make their plans, roping in others, conspiring to kill the King.

It was on his return to England that Thomas Winter renewed his acquaintance with the Spanish ambassador Juan Fernández de Velasco, Duke of Frias and Constable of Castile, who had come to negotiate an English treaty with Spain. Don Juan recognised Winter's claim that 3,000 men could be raised to fight the Catholics as being unrealistic. But after a meeting with King James, he did write to the Spanish government explaining the very great necessity to agree that a clause in a peace with England should include emancipation of the Catholics. [86]

Sometime in the June of the previous year, in his mother's house at Ashby St Leger, Catesby had been visited by his friend, the already mentioned Thomas Percy, great-grandson of the 4th Earl of Northumberland. As a young man Percy was described as 'very wild more than ordinary, and much given to fighting,'[87] who, having apparently deserted his wife, was imprisoned for killing a man while fighting on the Borders. Then, having converted to Catholicism, he had reputedly calmed down.

A tall man 'of serious expression but with an attractive manner' he suffered from some sort of skin complaint to the extent that 'he could not endure any shirt but of the finest fabric.'[88] Antonia Fraser writes 'that he sweated so much that he had to change his shirt three times a day.' Nonetheless, despite this unattractive complaint, having once converted to Catholicism, his relative Henry Percy, 9th Earl of Northumberland, had made him constable of Alnwick Castle, with responsibility for collecting the rents from his northern estates.

It was during this period, while the tenants complained of maladministration and bribery that Percy had killed the Scottish man, called James Burne, for which crime he had been thrown into a London jail. His release had then been arranged by the Earl of Essex, for whom he fought during yet another foray across the Scottish Border. Nevertheless, for reasons unspecified, he had not taken part in Essex's failed rebellion of 1601.

Subsequently in Flanders, Percy had fought for Northumberland during the latter's command, for which, on returning to England in 1603, the Earl had rewarded him by making him factor, or land agent, in Cumberland and Northumberland. On the strength of his fervent Catholicism, Northumberland had then entrusted Percy with secret correspondence with the Scottish King, who by that time seemed poised to succeed the dying Queen Elizabeth.

Exactly what Percy believed that James had then promised will never be known. 'The wisest fool in Christendom' was always circumspect in his dealings, but Percy, at least, believed that he had sworn to liberate the Catholics and had then reneged on the agreement. Percy then hated him to the extent, that after arriving in Lambeth, he told Catesby he would kill the King with his own hands. Catesby advised restraint, telling him, "I am thinking of a most sure way and I will soon let thee know what it is."[89]

Thus it was that Thomas Percy, 'the wild man from the north,' found himself amongst the five assembled, either in the inn called the Duck and Drake, close to the Strand, their favourite drinking place, or, as Professor Haynes believes and as seems more likely due to its secrecy, in a lodging belonging to a Mrs Herbert in Butcher's Row behind the church of St Clement Dane

Wherever their actual meeting place, it is certain that the others there were Catesby, his cousin Thomas Winter and Guy Fawkes, described as 'a tall, powerfully built man, with thick reddish brown hair, a flowing moustache in the tradition of the time, and a bushy reddish-brown beard.' [90] There too was Fawkes's former fellow pupil at St Peter's School in York, John Wright. The last named, married to Percy's sister Margaret, who, together with his brother Christopher was thought to be a dangerous religious fanatic, had been arrested and charged with conspiracy against Queen Elizabeth in 1596. Involved in the Essex rebellion in 1601, he had been imprisoned, as the Queen was dying, in 1603.

Wearing the high stove pipe hats, so fashionable at the time– Percy appears to have had a feather in his–and in doublets and breeches, the five sat huddled round a table. Firstly it was Percy, impatient as ever, who burst out with, "Shall we always, gentlemen, talk and never do anything?"[91] Catesby told him to be patient, saying that he and the others with him had not as yet formulated their plans. After some discussion all five of those present swore an oath of secrecy, their hands resting on a prayer book.

"Ye shall swear by the Blessed Trinity and by the Sacrament ye now prepare to receive never to disclose directly or indirectly by word or circumstances the matter that shall be proposed to you to keep secret nor to desist from the execution thereof until the rest shall give you leave."

Then adjoining to another room, they celebrated the mass and made their communion with Father Gerard, himself ignorant of their schemes, before, retiring back to the room of their meeting, Catesby disclosed their purpose to Thomas Percy, while Winter and John Wright told Fawkes of what was planned. [92]

CHAPTER 3
Betrayal

The next step forward came in June 1604, when Percy's appointment as a Gentleman Pensioner, provided an excuse for him to acquire a base in London. Thanks to Northumberland's agents, he subleased a house in Westminster from its tenant, a man called Henry Ferrers, where, once installed, calling him John Jonson, he made Fawkes his so-called servant. The bargaining for the house was finally completed on 24th May 1604. But the building could not be immediately occupied because the Scottish Commissioners, picked by King James to construct his scheme for the Union of Scotland and England, were already in occupation for several months.

Thwarted, the plotters had to make use of Catesby's house in Lambeth, on the south-side of the river, sited fortunately opposite the building rented from Ferrers, on the north-side of the Thames. Here they began operations by storing up gunpowder, wood and anything else that would burn, ready to be transferred by boat, under cover of darkness, to the opposite shore. Meanwhile, to act as guard, they enlisted Kit Wright, John Wright's brother.

It was at this point that Catesby roped in a fervent Jesuit, called Robert Keyes, red-headed and bearded described as 'a desperate man, ruined and indebted,' Catesby apparently paid him, and despite his reputation, believed him to be 'a trusty, honest man.'[93]

It was sometime early in the winter of 1604 that Catesby included his servant, Robert Bates,–who had somehow discovered what was happening–into the conspiracy, before shortly afterwards, enlisting Robert Winter (Thomas's brother) and the latter's brother-in-law John Grant. Both of these men were rich and well-known for hiding priests in their substantial houses.

In the first week of December, the Commission on the Treaty of Union finally finished its work allowing the conspirators to use Thomas Percy's rented house. Once in possession they began tunnelling through the walls separating the building from the House of Lords. It was gruelling work to men unused to manual labour, so that, after a few weeks, they had to draft in Robert Keyes, together with Christopher Wright. So too came the gunpowder of which Keyes had been left in charge, no less than 20 barrels of it now kept, either in Percy's rented house, or a garden shed nearby. By the middle of March they were half way through the main wall.

It was during a break in operations, perhaps when taking a breather as they were leaning on their picks, that they heard a noise in the room above.

Fawkes went up cautiously to see what it was. He found himself in a large room and realised, to his amazement, that it comprised the whole of the ground floor below the House of Lords. Hitherto let to a coal merchant, the noise turned out to be that of sacks of coal being dragged across the floor by men employed by the widow of the merchant, a Mrs Ellen Bright, selling-off what amounted to her husband's remaining stock.

Fawkes, when he looked round the room, once the kitchen of the original Palace of Westminster but now used as a cellar, could scarcely believe his luck. The place was filthy but empty, ideal for what he and his companions intended. They could stop tunnelling at once.

Following this, it was not until 25 March, in the following fateful year of 1605, that Percy actually contrived to acquire the lease for the undercroft, as the cellar was then described, so ideally placed, directly below the first floor containing the House of Lords. It was into this room that the plotters transferred 36 barrels of gunpowder, ferrying them by night across the river from Catesby's lodgings on the other side of the Thames.

On 9 June Father Henry Garnet met Robert Catesby in a room on Thames Street in London. Garnet, the Jesuit superior in England, was a devout and gentle man who constantly urged the English Catholics not to rise in rebellion. The son of a master of a grammar school in Nottingham, Garnet had gone on to study at

Winchester College where he had become a star pupil, noted in particular for his 'rare and delightful voice' and skill at playing the lute. Leaving the college, he had worked for a time for a publisher in London, before going to Rome to become a professor of Hebrew. He had returned to England at the urgent request of Father William Weston, the Jesuit superior, who, in their meeting had given him names of the Catholic houses that would shelter him, just before Weston himself was arrested on the capital charge of treachery, imposed upon all Jesuits since 1585. Garnet, although nearly caught several times, believed, nonetheless that it was his duty to watch in disguise the executions of priests, so as to secretly administer the last rites to them before they died. [94]

Then, in July there was a second meeting, this time at Fremland in Essex, when Catesby arrived with Lord Monteagle and the latter's cousin Francis Tresham. The priest, Father Garnet, was kept hidden in a secret room, but emerged from it, to walk in the long gallery. Strictly questioned by Catesby about the morality of entering into an unknown undertaking which might involve the deaths of innocent people, Garnet replied that such actions could often be excused, but later admonished Catesby, showing him a letter from the Pope, which firmly forbade rebellion. When Garnet felt brave enough to confront Lord Monteagle, he asked him directly if Catholics were able to make their part good by arms against the King, to which Garnet's only reply was that the King was 'odious to all.'

Plans were then put on hold, when, on the 28 of July, a further suspension of Parliament was announced due to the threat of the plague: a new date being fixed of 5 November.

Fawkes, who had gone abroad, returned in September to England. Reaching the house where the tunnelling was in progress, he found that some of the gunpowder had deteriorated, so that more had to be smuggled in. Other conspirators, were then recruited, amongst them Ambrose Rookwood, a young landowner in Suffolk, and Everard Digby, a rich young man with, most importantly, a fine stable of horses. Then finally, on 14 October, Francis Tresham, was brought into the plot.

Tresham, born about 1567, the eldest son of Sir Thomas Tresham and his wife Merial Throckmorton, was by then nearly forty. Having fought in the Earl of Essex's rebellion in 1601 he had been imprisoned and only his father's money had saved him from death and attainder. Despite this he had made two journeys to Spain to try to gain financial support for a Catholic rising in England.

According to Tresham's own confession, the meeting with Catesby took place at the home in Clerkenwell of his brother-in-law, Lord Stourton. Catesby asked him for money and the use of his family home Rushton Hall. The latter request was refused but Tresham, claiming himself to be in financial difficulty due to his father's debts, did give a small sum to Thomas Winter on the understanding that he was to travel to the Low Countries. Then, following the meeting, he rushed back to Rushton Hall to close the house and hide the family papers, before travelling again to London with his mother and sisters. Terrified of what was about to happen he contrived to obtain a licence to travel abroad with his servants and horses as late as 2 November.

By then the plan was fully organised. During the State Opening of Parliament, fixed for 5 November, when the King and his ministers were in attendance, they would blow them all to smithereens. Once this was accomplished they would kidnap Princess Elizabeth, the King's daughter, known to be living at Coombe Abbey in Warwickshire, and make her a titular queen.[95] Likewise, if Prince Henry, the Prince of Wales, escaped the explosion, Percy would capture him as well.

Percy returned to the north of England to collect his patron, Northumberland's rents, the conspirators intending to make the Earl the Lord Protector on the success of their plans. Meanwhile, in London, Catesby rallied more support. In all, with himself included, he had thirteen Catholic men pledged to his cause by October 1605.

On Saturday 25 October, Lord Monteagle was dining in his house in Hoxton, when outside a man described as 'reasonable tall, ' gave a letter, addressed to Monteagle, to one of his servants. Once opened, he discovered it to be a warning written by an unknown hand.

'My Lord out of the love I beare to some of youere frends I have a caer of youer preseruacion therfor I would advyse yowe as yowe tender youer lyf to devys some excuse to shift of youer attendance at this parleament for God and man hath concurred to punishe the wickedness of this time and think not slyghtlye of this advertisement but retyre youre self into youre contri wheare yowe may expect the event in safti for thowghe theare be no apparence of ani stir yet I saye they shall receive a terrible blowe this parliament and yet they shal not seie who hurts them this cowncel is not to be contemned because it maye do yowe good and can do yowe no harme for the danger is passed as soon as yowe have burnt the letter and I hope god will give yowe the grace to mak good use of it to whose holy proteccion I commend yowe.'[96]

Monteagle at once decided that the King must be warned. Calling for a horse, he rode through London in the dark to Whitehall where he found Robert Cecil, Lord Salisbury, together with the Earls of Worcester, Northampton and Suffolk sitting down to a late supper. They told him that the King was at Ware, where he had been hunting, but would be back in Whitehall the next day. Therefore they waited until James returned when, on reading the letter, the King was convinced that his English enemies meant to kill him by blowing him up with gunpowder, just as the Scottish men who hated his father had slaughtered him at Kirk O'Fields.

The secret was out but who betrayed it? Francis Tresham has long been suspected on the grounds of his concern for his cousin Lord Monteagle. But likewise there are other theories, including that of the whole thing being a conspiracy by the King's favourite minister, Robert Cecil, whom he had newly created Earl of Salisbury. Tresham had in fact left London when the mysterious letter was delivered, but returned on 30 October to join Catesby, Percy, Rookwood and Winter. Catesby employed Rookwood to buy some things that he needed while assuring him, categorically, that nothing concerning the plot had been discovered.[97]

But this was not the case. Thomas Winter had found out, through one of Monteagle's servants that the King and his closest councillors were considering what action to take over the anonymous letter. On Sunday, 3 November, Winter went to meet Tresham in the latter's house in Lincoln's Inn Walk and found him so distracted that he was left in little doubt as to his being the writer of the letter. Thomas Percy, a true descendant of 'Hotspur' refused to believe it and when some of the others suggested escaping abroad, he scoffed at the idea and reminded them of the boat lying at anchor in the Thames with a crew standing ready to draw anchor and take them to safety by sailing down the Thames.

Reluctantly, the group agreed to wait. Fawkes was to guard the gunpowder, still stacked in the cellar undisturbed, although by now, after six months in the confined space, showing signs of damp. Despite Percy's protest that they were unnecessary, some safety measures were taken and it was agreed, that while Percy himself and Winter would keep a watch throughout the city, Catesby and John Wright would hurry north to warn Digby and the other schemers to be ready to leave the country if anything went wrong.

The details of the plan were finalised. Everything hinged on the effects of the vast explosion, which would reverberate throughout the city. Then, in the aftershock, if the timing went right the next morning, the proclamation was to be read to all loyal Catholics to unite and seize control of the government and the country. With the King dead and most probably his eldest son Prince Henry killed in what was reckoned would be the total destruction of the House of Lords, the succession would pass to the five-year-old Prince Charles, or to the Princess Elizabeth who, as already intended, they would install as a Catholic queen.

But the letter sent to Lord Monteagle was ringing bells of alarm to the point where, on the afternoon of 4 November, Monteagle himself went with the Lord Chamberlain, the Earl of Suffolk, to make a search of the parliament buildings. With them was John Whynniard, yeoman of his Majesty's Wardrobe of the Beds, and owner of the property, rented so circumspectly to Henry Ferrers and sub-let to Thomas Percy in June of the previous year. After searching the Lord's Chamber they went down the stairs to the cellar which Whynniard had let to the coal merchant and subsequently to his widow, Mrs Bright, until she had sold off the business following her husband's death.

In the fading light of that November day, they almost missed it. But their eyes were somehow attracted by a large pile of faggots, which they walked around, no doubt prodding with their canes, as they tried to decipher their use. Then suddenly, lurking in the shadows, they spied a solitary man, who, saying he was a servant of Percy's, was in fact Guy Fawkes. The searchers left the cellar to report their findings and it was the King himself, who, after some discussion with his advisers, their suspicions definitely aroused, who ordered that another, more thorough search of the ground floor of the Parliament building should be made.

This time it was Sir Thomas Knyvett, a privy councillor and a Westminster magistrate, who led a strong armed group of men to make a more thorough investigation. They must have made a noise or shown a light as it was just approaching midnight when Guy Fawkes carefully opened the door to see what was going on. Immediately, Knyvett gave the order to seize him and his arms were bound behind his back. Seeing him secured, Knyvett, by the light of a lantern, then poked about amongst the faggots until, as some of them fell apart, he saw the barrels of gunpowder, unmistakeable for what they were.

Fawkes was immediately searched and concealed in pockets beneath his cloak, a watch, matches and touchwood –which later he said would have taken fifteen minutes to burn to give him time to escape the doomed building–were found. Amazed as these items were produced, Knyvett, gasping with excitement at the triumph of his discovery, then ran through the night to Whitehall Palace. There, the King, apparently still awake himself, had members of his privy council summoned and if necessary hauled out of bed, to attend an immediate meeting in his bedchamber to which Fawkes, pinioned as a felon, was taken for preliminary questioning at four o'clock in the morning of 5 November.

Fawkes, who gave his name as John Johnson, saying that he was a 36-year-old Catholic from Netherdale in Yorkshire and that his father was Thomas and his mother Edith Jackson, when first interrogated, remained defiant to the point where the King, in unwilling admiration, described him as being possessed with 'a Roman resolution' Admitting that it was his intention to blow up the House of Lords, and expressing his great regret at his failure to do so, when asked by one of the questioners why he was carrying so much gunpowder, Fawkes reputedly retorted 'to blow you Scotch beggars back to your native mountains.'[98]

The King's admiration, however, did not prevent him from ordering that Fawkes be tortured, albeit lightly at first with manacles but more severe if he remained obdurate to the point where the rack, if necessary, could be used. Sir William Waad, Lieutenant of the Tower, supervised the proceedings. A letter addressed to Guy Fawkes was found concealed on his person but he still persisted in saying that his name was John Johnson while refusing adamantly to reveal the identity of any of his fellow conspirators.

On the following day, 7 November, in agony from the torture, Fawkes confessed to his true name and admitted that there were five men involved in the attempt to kill the King. Then, on the following day, he owned up as to how, on the death of her father and presumably her elder brother Prince Henry, they had meant to make the Princess Elizabeth queen and on the day after that he gave his interrogators the name of Francis Tresham. His words, dictated to a scribe, were signed at the foot of each page, at first Guido Fawkes with a strong hand before in the last instance the single word Guido, by then almost illegible, distorted beyond comprehension, by the suffering he had by that time been forced to endure.[99]

CHAPTER 4
Stand By Me, Mr Tom

As day dawned on Tuesday 6 November Thomas Winter, sleeping in the Duck and Drake in the Strand, was shaken awake by John, youngest of the Wright brothers, to be told of Guy Fawkes' arrest. Winter then sent him running to find Thomas Percy, to tell him to leave London with all possible speed.

Winter himself was determined to stay and see things through. Going to the Court Gates he found them heavily guarded against anyone wishing to enter. From there he headed towards the buildings of the Parliament but found himself confronted by a soldier, barring his way with sword and pike.

Returning towards the inn he overheard a by-passer telling someone else 'there is treason discovered, in which the King and the Lords should have been blown up' and knew the plot to be disclosed.

While Winter lingered in London, waiting to see what would occur, Robert Catesby, the man behind the whole conspiracy, was riding for his life into the country. Leaving the city at about eleven, he spurred on his horse, covering 80 miles in seven hours.

The horses provided by Ambrose Rookwood, saddled and bridled, waited at pre-arranged meeting places along the way. Rookwood himself, on a thoroughbred, overtook him, together with John Wright who had joined him, beyond the small Bedfordshire town of Brickhill. A few miles on they found Thomas Percy and Christopher Wright and the five men rode on together at a speed so desperate that Percy and John Wright threw their heavy and expensive cloaks into a hedge to lighten the weight for their steeds.

Reaching Dunchurch, at an inn called The Lion, they found about a hundred Catholic supporters who had assembled from the surrounding country uncertain of what action was intended.

Told of the desperate situation most of them quickly dispersed leaving only about forty of the braver souls to try to plan ways of escape.

Amongst those who stayed was John Wright, who, at midnight had led a party of others to raid the stables at Warwick Castle taking nine or ten horses out of their stables, leaving their own tired ones in their place. The whole party, well-armed with muskets, then rode on fording the river Alne to reach Alcester and then along the Worcester road and from thence by country lanes until, at about two o'clock on the afternoon of Wednesday 7 November, both men and horses exhausted, they reached the home of the Winters, Huddington Court.

Some six miles east of the town of Worcester, the 15th century manor house of Huddington, black and white with black beams prominent against the white painted walls, stands surrounded by a moat. Within the house itself are no less than three priest holes, the first on the ground floor, where from beneath a floorboard a spiral staircase runs down to a room below. The second is of a bedroom on the top floor, where a set of bricks, cleverly disguised, could be pulled out to reveal a hole large enough for a man to crawl through into a room so low that, while it could hold four men, it was impossible to stand. The third can only be reached from the room above through a disguised panel in the wall, which could be removed and replaced on the other side. In the main bedroom, etched into a pane in the glass with her diamond ring are the words 'Passed cark, passed care' carved by Thomas Winter's wife, as she stood, probably trembling, gazing out towards the woods where she knew her husband was hiding as the soldiers searched.

It was only on the evening of the 7th that Thomas Winter himself reached his home, his brother John, in the meanwhile setting guards on all the roads. With the others he slept until three o'clock in the morning, when in the cold of the November night, they were woken by the women in the house to attend the Mass conducted by Father Nicholas Hart, who heard the confessions of men who knew they were soon likely to die. Then in the hall they found arms, armour and ammunition laid out on long tables, from which they selected their choice, before the rest were placed in carts for transportation.

It was at about six, in the first light of dawn, that the whole party moved off intending to reach Wales where there was strong Catholic support. But now outriders came in with the bad news that that the sheriff of Worcestershire, Sir Richard Walsh, with a large party of soldiers was on their tail. Frustrated, both by the weather and the slowness of the oxen-pulled carts, they could not move fast over roads that were deep in mud, resulting from recent heavy rain. Unfortunately, due to flooding, some of the gunpowder got wet as they were fording the flooded River Stour.

To make matters worse, men disheartened and frightened by news of the Sheriff's approach, were deserting, so that it was a greatly reduced party that, once again in darkness, reached Holbeach House, belonging to Stephen Littleton, at about ten o' clock at night.

From there, early the next morning, spurred on by near desperation, Thomas Winter set off with Stephen Littleton to try to persuade the nearby landowner, Sir John Talbot, owner of the estate of Pepperhill, to help them.

But Talbot adamantly refused, telling Winter rudely to be gone. Dispirited, he and Littleton returned to Holbeach only to find that a horrible accident had occurred. Some of the wet gunpowder had been put on wooden platters to dry before the fire. A stray spark had fallen onto one of them and caused an explosion. A man called John Grant was blinded and both Robert Catesby, Ambrose Rookwood and Grant's friend Henry Morgan, horribly burned. Ironically, the man who had planned to destroy the King by gunpowder had all but perished in the same way himself.

On discovering what had happened, Robert Winter and Stephen Littleton both left the house to hide in the woods. Thomas Winter most resolute of friends, however, stayed in the house to try to dress and bandage the wounds of the injured men. Knowing that escape was hopeless, as from the windows he saw the Sheriff's men converge, he then began to try and organise an inadequate but heroic defence of Holbeach house.

At 11 o' clock the next morning the attackers surrounded the building. Somehow they started a fire, perhaps with flaming arrows shot into the roof. Then, with a roar of triumph, they either charged over the bridge spanning the moat, or crossed by boat to hammer down the door.

For those left within the house there was no escape. Thomas Winter was shot in the shoulder, Christopher Wright, and his brother John were killed, gunned down in the courtyard, and Ambrose Rookwood, already injured by the explosion, was wounded. But Winter, although hurt, managed to crawl back into the house to find Robert Catesby and Thomas Percy still uninjured.

"Stand by me Mr Tom," said Catesby to Percy, "and we will die together."

The three men, knowing that all hope of rescue was gone, stepped out as one from behind the door, behind which they had been sheltering, to face, what they knew to be, certain death. Robert Catesby, Thomas Percy and Thomas Winter, standing together, were all killed, Catesby and Percy reputedly by a single shot. But the legend lives that Catesby, badly wounded, just found the strength to drag himself back to the house, where, with a picture of the Virgin Mary clutched to his heart, he died.

Thus ended the life of the man, who of all would-be assassins, made the most determined and organised attempt to kill King James. The King himself was petrified, if what Nicolò Molin, the Venetian ambassador wrote is true.

'The King is in terror, he does not appear nor does he take his meals in public as usual. He lives in the innermost rooms with only Scotchmen [sic] about him…Catholics fear heretics and vice versa…both are armed: foreigners live in terror of their houses being sacked by the mob which is convinced that some, if not all foreign princes, are at the bottom of the plot. The King and council have very prudently thought it advisable to quiet the popular feeling by issuing a proclamation in which they declare that no foreign Sovereign had any part in the conspiracy.' [100]

CHAPTER 5
The Gallow's Net

Terrified as was the King, his fear must have been magnified in the minds of the conspirators as they were rounded up one by one.

Of those who escaped from Holbeach House, just before it was stormed, Sir Everard Digby, the rich young man inveigled into the plot because of his fine string of horses, was soon captured together with two servants, thought to have been Thomas Bates (the man employed by Catesby who had inadvertently discovered the plot) and his son. Once made prisoner they were taken up to London to the Tower.

Meanwhile John Winter, who had escaped from Holbeach, decided to beg for the King's mercy but a search went out, throughout the surrounding country, for his brother Robert, and Stephen Littleton, owner of the house. Given sanctuary by Stephen's brother Humphrey Littleton, they were all betrayed for money by the latter's cook and joined the other prisoners in the Tower.

The trial of the prisoners, brought by barge from the Tower to the Palace of Westminster, took place at the end of January 1606. As they waited in the Star Chamber, some stood with heads bowed but others were smoking as if 'they did not mind being hanged.'[101]

Digby, in the short speech that was all that was allowed to him, said that he had joined the conspiracy for three reasons. The first was for his great affection for Catesby, the man for whose famous charm he had been ready to risk his life. Secondly, it was for his religion and thirdly for the real reason that fired so much animosity, namely the King's broken promises to the Catholics and for the prevention of the ever more stringent laws against them for which they lived in such fear.

The Earl of Northampton, in a long-winded speech, stoutly defended the monarch against all of Digby's claims of his having broken his word, before, as was expected, the jury found all the prisoners guilty and the Lord Chief Justice, Sir John Popham proclaiming them all guilty of high treason, condemned them to death.

Digby, Robert Winter, John Grant and Thomas Bates were roped onto wattled hurdles at the Tower to be dragged on their backs, for the mile to the scaffold in St Paul's churchyard. Digby, showed great courage, his last words being, "O Jesus, Jesus, save me and keep me," as he climbed up the ladder to the platform from which he was hanged.

The next day Thomas Winter, Robert Keyes, Ambrose Rookwood and finally, Guy Fawkes, were all executed. Fawkes, due to torture on the verge of collapse, so weak that he could hardly walk, still managed to jump from the scaffold, breaking his neck in the fall, thus avoiding the agony of disembowelment while still alive, which the others were forced to endure. [102]

Of the rest involved in the conspiracy, Francis Tresham claimed that he was guilty only of the plot's concealment, He assured his inquisitors that he had persuaded Thomas Winter and Thomas Percy to postpone the intended explosion and that he had been on the point of informing the King's secretary, Thomas Lake, of the plot. In the meantime, all thoughts of Tresham's trial were postponed as, suffering from a strangury caused by inflammation of his urinary tract, he became terminally ill. So great was his suffering that the Lieutenant of the Tower, Sir William Waad, took pity on him, allowing him to be attended by no less than four doctors and eventually a nurse. Aware that he was dying, Tresham apologised to Father Henry Garnet for implicating him in the attempt to get money to finance a Catholic rising from Spain. He died on 23 December, after which, despite through his illness having escaped a trial, his head was displayed beside those of Catesby and Percy, while his body was thrown into a hole at Tower Hill. His letter of apology to Henry Garnet, together with one of the priest's own, explaining the reasons for his Equivocation, was found in his chamber in the Inner Temple and used with great effect in the trial of Father Garnet by the Attorney-General, Sir Edward Coke.

Father Garnet had been at Coughton Hall, near Alcester in Warwickshire, when Thomas Bates, brother of John, brought news of the plot's disastrous failure. The house had been rebuilt round a courtyard in the Tudor style, in the previous reign of Queen Elizabeth by Sir George Throckmorton, whose family had owned it since 1409. Like others possessed by Catholics in the neighbourhood, it had a priest hole in which Garnet may have been hiding when Bates came with his terrible news.

Following this, Father Garnet spent several weeks moving from one safe house to another until, towards the end of January, he reached Hindlip Hall, another large house, this time owned by Sir Thomas Abingdon whose wife Mary, was the sister-in-law of Lord Monteagle. Apparently, it was Humphrey Littleton who informed the authorities that Father Edward Oldcorne was hiding there after he had been heard saying Mass in the house. Certainly Garnet was with Father Oldcorne when they hid themselves in a small space, so cramped that they were unable even to stand up or stretch their legs. Food and drink they received from their protectors, through a small drinking straw hidden within the structure of the building But of any form of sanitation there was none so that, forced by 'customs of nature which must of necessity be done' they had to emerge from hiding whereupon they were immediately captured by spies who were watching or hiding within the house.

Taken first to Holt Castle in Worcestershire, they were then moved on to London. Garnet was still weak from his incarceration in the priest hole but Lord Salisbury, in unexpected compassion, ordered that he be given a horse that was easy to ride, while his supplies were paid for by the King. With them went a Puritan minister, who 'ranted at length without interruption' but Garnet, much to the man's annoyance, tempered his outbursts with replies that were both academic and clear. On reaching London the priest was taken to the Gatehouse Prison in Westminster where many Catholics, amongst them his nephew Thomas Garnet, were held.

Father Henry Garnet appeared before the Privy Council on 13 February 1606. His questioners included the Chief Justice, Sir John Popham, the Attorney-General Sir Edward Coke, Sir William Waad, Lieutenant of the Tower, Robert Cecil, Earl of

Salisbury, Secretary to the King, and the Howard Earls of Northampton and Nottingham.

Initially they treated the elderly priest with respect, doffing their hats and addressing him as Mr Garnet. But they ridiculed his relationship with Anne Vaux, the heiress daughter of Lord Vaux, a relation of Catesby's, and committed Jesuit in whose house called White Webbs, at Enfield, they had often foregathered, calling him her lover rather than her confessor. His own doctrine on equivocation, was then laid out on a table before him to be condemned by the council as 'one of the heretical, treasonable and damnable books' found in Francis Tresham's collection.

The next day, however, Garnet was moved, into what he himself described as 'a very fine chamber' in the Tower, where, renowned as he was for his love of good wine, he was even given claret with his meals. Nonetheless it was all part of a scheme to gain his trust and thereby incriminate himself. To further this purpose, his jailer, a man named Carey, transferred him to a cell with a hole in the wall through which he could talk, or rather whisper, to Father Oldcorne while two government listeners heard every word that they said. His letters, both to his nephew and to Anne Vaux, written in orange juice, were also intercepted and read by Waad who kept Salisbury informed of their contents both innocent and otherwise. Anne Vaux was arrested and questioned twice. She admitted to sheltering Catholics in her house, but insisted she was innocent of treason and thanks to a bond put up by a man called Lewis Pickering, some six months later she was released.

Garnet, most likely under torture, eventually allowed that, although horrified as he is known to have been over Catesby's plan, he had been aware of the plot to kill the King and the members of his Government by blowing up the House of Lords. It was enough to condemn him as a traitor.

His trial took place on Friday 28 March 1606. He was taken to the Guildhall in a closed coach, equivalent of the police van of today, a precaution taken by the government for fear of the sympathy of the crowds who lined the streets to watch. Proceedings began at about 9.30 a.m. with the King and Lady Arbella Stuart, James's main contender for the throne, who, as

Queen Anne's main train-bearer, was then living at the court, watching hidden from view.

Accused of having conspired with Catesby, on 9 June 1605 (their first meeting) to kill the King, his son, and 'to alter and subvert the government of the kingdom and the true worship of God established in England,' and of conspiring with several others to blow up the House of Lords with gunpowder, Garnet pleaded not guilty, his defence that he had forbidden Catesby to proceed with his intention being ignored. The jury took only a quarter-of-an-hour to declare him culpable of high treason and sentenced him to be hanged, drawn and quartered, the dreadful death given to traitors at the time.

On Saturday 3 May, strapped to a hurdle, Garnet was drawn by three horses to the churchyard of St Paul's Cathedral. He died, reaffirming his innocence. But before the executioner could cut him down what the authorities had feared took place as people in the watching crowd surged forward to pull down his feet and break his neck, thus sparing him the final torture of being disembowelled. As the executioner held up his heart, proclaiming it that of a traitor, there was silence, instead of the usual applause. Nonetheless, when his head was set on a pole on London Bridge so many gaped in horror at the pallor of the skin that the government ordered the face to be turned upwards so as to be no longer visible to sight.

CHAPTER 6
Poison and Beauty Intertwined

And so died the peace-loving priest who had shied away in horror from the very thought of the scheme which Catesby, forceful enough to bend men's minds with his charm, had set before him. King James, the intended victim, was to live for almost another twenty years from the date on which the attempt to blow him to pieces was planned. During that time he was spared both physical attack and attempts to kill him by other means. Instead it was the conniving of two women, one impetuous and stupid, the other a murderess, which threatened the stability of his rule.

The first of the two was his cousin, Arbella Stuart, the girl who, on his first arrival in England, had been cleared of all involvement in what was called the Main Plot, a Catholic conspiracy to replace him with Arbella on the throne.

The daughter of James' uncle Charles Stuart, (his father Henry Darnley's younger brother) who had married Elizabeth Cavendish, daughter of Sir William Cavendish and his redoubtable wife, Bess of Hardwick, Arbella was highly excitable and prone to bouts of hysteria, which some historians believe to have been porphyria. She was, nonetheless physically attractive with her fair skin and flaxen hair.

Orphaned at the age of seven, by the early death of her parents, the girl had been raised and ruled by her grandmother, at Chatsworth in Derbyshire, and her other houses elsewhere, until Bess herself had died in 1608.

Two years later, in 1610, Arbella, then free of her grandmother's influence, and politically important as fourth in line to the throne, was planning to marry William Seymour, a young man twelve years younger than herself, who, as the great-grandson of Henry VII's youngest daughter, the beautiful Mary,

Countess of Suffolk, was thus sixth in line to the throne. It was evident to James, that because of their combined relationships, they posed a threat to himself. The Catholic nobility might well renew their attempt to usurp him and to put the young couple on the throne.

For this reason the King, who had formerly shown his cousin much kindness, making her chief trainbearer, to Queen Anne, forbade her to marry William Seymour. Nonetheless, defiant of the consequences, they did marry secretly at Greenwich Palace on 22 June 1610.

The result was predictable. No one could defy the King. King James had them both arrested and imprisoned, Arbella in a house belonging to Sir Thomas Perry, in Lambeth and Seymour in the Tower of London They were, however, allowed some freedom and Arbella spent much of her time writing, both to King James and to her new husband, on the discovery of which James ordered her to be sent into the custody of William James, the Bishop of Durham.

But a day after leaving London, Arbella, either feigning illness or genuinely unwell, was taken to a house at Barnet. From there she got in touch with William, with whom she devised a plan to escape by ship from Blackhall in June. Time passed and she recovered, but a few days before she was supposed to continue her journey to Durham, she slipped out of the house in Barnet, disguised as a man and rode to London.

Arriving, she waited impatiently as William's plan to escape from the Tower, for some reason failed. Panicking, she sailed with the tide, persuading the captain of the ship to linger in the Channel waiting for him to catch up with her. But he failed to do so, somehow reaching France eventually on his own.

Meanwhile, sadly, Arbella's delay, proved fatal. Recaptured by a naval pinnace, sent out to find her, she returned a prisoner to the Tower of London.

There, within the Bell Tower she remained. The King, hurt and angry by what he thought to be her betrayal after his kindness to her and believing rumours of her involvement in a Catholic plot to seize his throne, never forgave her. Spared any form of trial, but realizing she would remain a prisoner for life, she lost the will to live. Refusing food and medication when she was ill, the woman who, had circumstances been otherwise, through her royal descent might have been Queen of Great Britain, died in September 1615 aged only thirty-nine.

Throughout the next two decades James and his Danish Queen Anne, who had converted to Catholicism, lived in a state of discord, which resulted eventually in them keeping separate establishments. Nevertheless they drew together in sorrow when their eldest son, the athletic, talented Prince Henry, died on 6 November 1612 from typhoid, caught by swimming in the Thames.

Prince Henry, according to his tutor Sir Charles Cornwallis, was different from his father in almost every aspect of his character. Whereas James detested everything connected with warfare, Henry, a young man of middle height with auburn hair, a piercing grave eye, a most gracious smile and terrible frown, totally bored by hunting and likewise his father's passion for books, wanted only to be a soldier. Training himself to endure hardship, he reputedly spent up to six hours a day wearing armour. Greatly interested in the navy, he hero-worshipped the imprisoned Sir Walter Raleigh saying that 'only his father would keep such a bird in a cage.'

James, while still in Scotland, had begun trying to find a suitable bride for his eldest son and in 1611 he reopened negotiations between the hugely rich Duke Cosmo II of Tuscany for the hand of his sister Caterina. But the Pope sternly forbade the match, stipulating both that Henry should become a Catholic and that English Catholics be allowed full liberty of worship before he would permit the marriage to take place.

Then came an offer from Charles Emmanuel, the Duke of Savoy of his daughter, the beautiful Infanta, much praised for her loveliness by Sir Henry Wotton who, travelling through Savoy caught a glimpse of her riding in a sledge. Another suggestion was that of the French Princess Christina, at that time only six. But Henry would have none of them saying that 'my part, to be in love with them is not yet at hand.'[103] His only real love was his sister Elizabeth. 'Where is my dear sister?' were his last words just before he died.

Princess Elizabeth, described by the courtier, Sir Henry Wotton as 'a most endearing girl, graceful, athletic and playful, spontaneous and high-spirited, prettily impulsive, generous and affectionate and possessed of engaging charm,' had in fact been occupied in meeting her future husband, Frederick, the Elector of the Palatinate, who had arrived in England on 16 October, as Henry's condition grew worse.

King James was delighted with his prospective son-in-law, discovering that he was almost as well-learned in both Latin and theology as himself. Frederick, in comparison to his own eldest son was in fact a model of virtue. But James, who could not force himself to come to his bedside, was utterly distraught when Henry died.

Although fifteen years had passed since the publication of his book on *Daemonologie* in 1597, King James was still obsessed with witchcraft in all its forms. His book, comprising three volumes, begins with the following words.

'The fearful aboundings at this time in this countrie, of these detestable slaves of the Devil, the Witches or enchanters, hath moved me (beloved reader) to dispatch in post, this following treatise of mine...to resolve the doubting...both that such assaults of Satan are most certainly practised, and that the instrument thereof merits most severely to be punished.'

The King then set out his theory that the Devilish arts have always existed, attributing some of the blame to biblical teachings and elaborates his views against papistry. He explains that he chose to write the book in the form of a dialogue–a common practice at the time–to make it an easier read. Philomathes hears news regarding the spread of witchcraft and discusses his views with another philosopher Epistemon, a recognised expert on theology. The King then sets out a scholarly explanation of all things that these include and the natural cause of the Devil's power with the use of philosophical reasoning. Explaining the justification of a witch trial, he details the awful punishments which a practitioner of the dark arts could expect.

Unsurprisingly, given his known obsession with witchcraft, King James took a great personal interest in the famous assizes at Lancaster in the autumn of 1612. At a time when there were few doctors and those who did exist had to be paid, most country people relied on the local 'wise women' who treated their illnesses with potions usually concocted of herbs. Most of these old dames were harmless, in fact beneficial to people who had no other remedies at hand. But some exercised the powers of magic, invoking curses, which perhaps through sheer co-incidence, caused harm or even death to those against whom they bore spite. Such was the power of some, known to have achieved their object, that people lived in terror of what was believed to be their evil eye.

In the case of the notorious Pendle Witch trials no less than twenty people, sixteen of them women of various ages, were committed to the court at Lancaster, some being held in the dungeons of Lancaster Castle to await their fate. Known collectively as the Witches of Pendle Forest and the Witches of Samiesbury they numbered eighteen women and two men of whom only four were discharged as innocent. Twelve who were charged with the murders of ten people by the use of magic, included two women who were accused of such horrid crimes as child murder and cannibalism. One harridan, a woman called Alizon Device of Pendle, blamed for causing a stroke by witchcraft, freely confessed that she had sold her soul to the Devil. Her daughter, a child of nine called Jennet, was a key witness for the prosecution giving evidence against her own family. This would not have been allowed in many other trials of the times, but because King James had made a case for suspending the normal rules of evidence for witchcraft trials in his *Daemonologie,* it was allowed.

The trials were a cause of nationwide sensation. Thousands of his subjects shared the King's fascination in all that was taking place. Notorious amongst those on trial were two very old women. One was the Witch Demdike, now at least eighty years old, who had been practising her craft for fifty years. Living deep in the Forest of Pendle, she had raised both her children and grandchildren to be witches. Feared as an agent for the Devil, it was claimed that no man, woman nor child escaped her or her furies and certain it was that no one near them felt safe or free from danger. The second old woman Anne Chattox, very withered and almost blind, muttering to herself as she moved, was a deadly rival of the first. Unlike many so called witches who brewed concoctions to heal the sick, these two outdid each other in making mischief to people's possessions, such as a cow going dry–then a calamity for most families–and in the case of a woman called Margaret Pearson, killing a horse. Thus through sheer malevolence did these old and largely infirm women–apparently in fierce competition with each other–held their power over the local country people.

Eventually in this most notorious of trials, nine women and two men found guilty of practising witchcraft, were executed by hanging, a fate evidently justified in the superstitious mind of the King.

But it was not some poor old hag from the Forest of Pendle in Lancashire, who, while the trials were still on progress in that autumn of 1612, became the second woman to threaten King James personally with the danger of complicity in a plan of lethal revenge. This time, unlike his poor reckless cousin Arbella, whose attraction had gone before she died, it was a young woman, whose beautiful face concealed a devious and criminal mind, who became of great danger to the King.

It may have been due to his desperate search for consolation, following the death of his son, that James gave so much affection to and became increasingly under the influence of the young man who had already contrived to inveigle himself into favouritism, named Robert Carr.

The younger son of Sir Thomas Kerr (Carr as it was spelt in England) of Ferniehurst in Scotland, Robert was actually born in Somerset in 1587. Aged about fourteen, in 1601, while a page to George Hume, Earl of Dunbar, he got to know Sir Thomas Overbury in Edinburgh. A friendship developed between them and they travelled together to London to seek their fortune in the wake of the new King, as did so many Scotsmen at that time. Whether their relationship was homosexual is unknown, but certainly Robert Carr's rather effeminate good looks and Overbury's over possessiveness would indicate that this was so.

Carr won success through an accident, being unlucky enough to break his leg in a tilting match just as he, with his fair hair and boyish good looks had caught the eye of the monarch who happened to be amongst the spectators. James, on the word of the Earl of Suffolk, was instantly captivated, visiting him while still incapacitated and teaching him Latin. The King, on his recovery, knighted him and made him a member of his court. The next step was to find him a property. Sir Walter Raleigh, detained for his involvement in the Main Plot, had lost his life-interest in the manor of Sherborne, in Warwickshire. Lord Salisbury assured the King that he was perfectly entitled to give it to Carr on which advice the manor was transferred to him and Carr took possession immediately. His rise to fame had begun. On 24 March 1611, he became Viscount Rochester and subsequently a Privy Councillor.

In 1612, on the death of Robert Cecil (Earl of Salisbury since 1605) the Howard families in England virtually took control of the government. Robert Carr, whom James had hoped to make his Chief Minister of State, found himself over-ruled and, for lack of experience, largely depended on Overbury for dealing with official papers.

Thomas Howard, son of the 4th Duke of Norfolk, who, having commanded the Lion in the fleet that sailed to vanquish the Spanish Armada, had become an admiral, had then been raised to the peerage as the Earl of Suffolk by James in 1603. Thereafter Lord Chamberlain, until 1614, his family dominated the court. Suffolk with his wife Katherine Knyvet, the widow of Lord Rich, herself a noted beauty, whom he married in 1582, had a large family of no less than seven sons and five daughters. Fifth of the daughters was Frances, said to have been bewitchingly lovely, who, at the age of fourteen, was forced into a marriage with Robert Devereux, who since his father's execution after his failed rebellion, had become the 3rd Earl of Essex at the age of ten and at the time of his marriage was only thirteen.

Kept apart, being thought too young for the marriage to be consummated, Essex then went on a tour throughout Europe, as was becoming the fashionable thing to do. It was during his fortuitous absence that Robert Carr, not yet ennobled but high in the King's favour, saw his chance to align himself to the Howard's ruling power.

The young Frances, now Countess of Essex, is said to have fallen in love with Carr, which in all probability she did. Certainly it is on record, that once her husband returned, seriously ill with small-pox, she refused to have anything to do with him.

Then followed one of the great scandals of the time, notorious even in King James's court, immoral as that was known to be. Frances demanded an annulment of her marriage, claiming that she had made every attempt to be sexually compliant to her husband but that thanks to his impotence she was still a virgin. Essex claimed that he could perfectly well make love to other women but was physically repelled by his wife, an argument that, in view of her exalted attraction, was hard to sustain. Frances' father and her great uncle, Henry Howard, Earl of Northampton, represented her in court where the judges decided, that in view of the extraordinary circumstances, satanic magic must have been involved. Essex was told to go to Poland to see if the curse could be lifted by demoniac means.

Frances Essex, desperate to be rid of her husband so that she could marry Robert Carr, turned for help to a woman called Anne Turner, whom she called her friend. A widow and apparently respectable, Anne Turner had gained access to the court from her business of selling a saffron-based starch which turned collars and cuffs yellow, a colour then all the rage in fashionable London.

Reputedly, however, she ran brothels through which she met some of the more doubtful members of London society, amongst them an apothecary called Simon Forman, thought to have been the model for *The Alchemist*, the famous play by Ben Jonson. Forbidden to practice medicine in London by the College of Physicians, Forman had retired to Lambeth, out with the limits of the city, where he ran a flourishing trade in providing love potions amongst many other concoctions. Frances, going in secret to visit him, reputedly returned with a lead figurine of a copulating couple, supposedly imbued with magic to stimulate Robert Carr, as well as some of the famous love potions which Anne Turner bribed Carr's servants to slip into his food and drink.

This was not all she acquired. Mr Forman then made a wax model of her husband into which Frances thrust thorns into the groin, believing by sorcery, to effect impotence, while at the same time giving him potions to increase the effect.

Frances then loudly proclaimed that her marriage had not been consummated. Submitting herself to examination by a party of midwives, she claimed that she was still a virgin and persuaded her Howard great-uncle, the Earl of Northampton, to use his influence with the King to get her marriage to Essex annulled.

Sir Thomas Overbury, who had done everything possible to prevent Robert Carr's absorption by the Howards, was incandescent with rage. Unsuccessfully he tried, by every means he knew, to rekindle their former friendship, but the Howards and their newly achieved acolyte, had no time for the likes of Overbury in their ruthless pursuit of power. Finding him a nuisance in his constant attempts to regain his old intimacy with his former protégé, they somehow contrived to accuse him of showing disrespect to Queen Anne. Then to get rid of him, they persuaded the ever quiescent King to offer him a position as ambassador to the court of Tsar Michael of Russia.

Predictably Overbury refused the post, whereupon, accused of treason, in April 1613, he was sent a prisoner to the Tower.

Once Overbury was safely encased within the stone walls of the prison, Henry Howard, the Earl of Northampton, still manipulative at the age of seventy-three, contrived that one of his agents, a man named Gervaise d'Elwes, be made Lieutenant of the Tower. This meant that his great-niece Frances, still then the Countess of Essex, had been able to install one of her own servants, a man called Richard Weston, to be in charge of Overbury. Frances then once more intrigued with Mrs Turner who, through another apothecary called Franklin, procured a variety of poisonous substances including arsenic, catharnides and sublimate of mercury. Surprisingly, she would seem to have been unaware that her lover, Robert Carr, presumably from a guilty conscience, feeling compassion for his old friend and mentor, was supplying him with various enemas and purgatives with the purpose of making him look so ill that the authorities might set him free. This of course had the effect of counter-acting the insidious poisons supplied to Overbury by Robert's wife. But Frances, desperate to get rid of the unfortunate man, then concocted a lethal dose of sublimate of mercury, which administered by her servant Weston, resulted in Overbury's agonizing and protracted death.

Overbury died on 15 September 1613, of natural causes, or so it was publicly proclaimed. Blisters on his skin were suggestive of syphilis, then a widespread disease. But few believed this explanation. The circumstances and method of his death were all too obviously contrived.

It soon transpired that Frances, still at this point the Countess of Essex, concerned for his state of health as she claimed, had been sending him jellies, nutritious as she insisted them to be. But those who were with him, to their horror, saw some of the jellies turn green. Overbury's condition had worsened quickly, ending in severe stomach pains before he died. Plainly he had been poisoned. Rumour spread quickly, that the benevolent countess was to blame.

Frances remained oblivious to the calumnies of which she was accused. James would do anything to please his beloved Robert Carr. The King, still in thrall to his favourite, did everything to help his cause. On 25 September, just ten days after Overbury's death, Robert Earl of Essex, backed by the royal authority, won a decree of nullity against his wife.

On 3 November James gave Carr the earldom of Somerset, before, on 23 December, making him Treasurer of Scotland. Then, six weeks later, on 26 December, Frances Countess of Essex, the former Frances Howard, married the newly created earl to become, for the second time a countess, this time of Somerset.

Unaccountably two years went by before the Countess of Suffolk was summoned to face justice for her crime. During this time her husband remained in high favour with King James, from whom further honours continued to appear. But in 1615 a new star appeared at court when, at a hunt in Northamptonshire, George Villiers, described as 'the handsomest-bodied man in all of England; his limbs so well compacted, and his conversation so pleasing, and of so sweet a disposition,' [104] caught the King's eye. This gave Somerset's enemies their chance. Seeing a way to displace him, they contrived to make James appoint the young Villiers, first as a royal cupbearer and then as a Gentleman of the Bedchamber in which position he was constantly in contact with the King.

In 1615, James, entranced with his new favourite, made a list of complaints against Somerset, who might have survived had it not been that, in July, the poisoning of Overbury was revealed.

This came about in a way that no one, least of all Frances Somerset, could have foreseen. Confident that she had got away with her crime, she was unaware that some people still existed who knew far too much about how it had been achieved.

Amongst them was a man of such little significance that she may not have known of his existence. His name was William Reeve, who, as assistant to the apothecary Franklin, had acted under his instruction when preparing the lethal poisons with which the countess had been supplied. Following the death of Overbury, Reeve, probably on Northampton's order, had been sent to France.

But there he had taken ill and believing he was close to death had confessed to being the man who had delivered the deadly poisons, aimed as he guessed, at the death of a prisoner, to the Tower of London. Pressed by those around his bedside, he had then revealed the names of those involved in the murder of Sir Thomas Overbury.

The news in France of a sensational *crime passionnel,* spread across the Channel with the speed of a pursuing wind. King James, horrified, tried to ignore it, until told that it was now being rumoured that he himself had ordered the killing of Overbury at the instigation of, the Earl of Somerset, no longer the prime favourite, and his beautiful but scheming wife.

Once again, as when within a locked room he had found himself facing the naked steel of Alexander Ruthven's sword, the King was convulsed with terror. Facing up to it, he ordered the chief justice, Sir Edward Coke, to investigate the claim that Overbury had been done to death by poison.

Coke acted quickly. Robert Weston, Frances' servant and her friend Anne Turner, together with Gervase d'Elwes, appointed by Northampton Overbury's keeper in the Tower, and Simon Franklin, the alchemist, were all arrested and brought to trial. All four were found guilty of complicity in Overbury's murder, condemned to death and hanged.

Then excitement amongst the populace of London grew as the Earl and Countess of Somerset were summoned before the court on a similar charge of murder. Frances Somerset, already too incriminated to deny it, confessed to her involvement in the crime and pleaded guilty. Her husband insisted on his innocence but, on the overwhelming evidence, both were condemned to death.

Neither sentence was carried out. King James, apparently, still had some affection for his former beloved friend and may even have believed in his sworn innocence of any attempt to harm Overbury. In the event both the Somersets were imprisoned in the Tower until freed, Frances in 1622 and Robert Somerset two years later in 1624.

But, on their release, there was no returning to the court. Forced to retire to the country, to Rotherfield Greys in Oxfordshire, they lived, hardly on speaking terms with each other, at opposite ends of the house. Frances died, probably of ovarian cancer in 1652 and Robert survived her for thirteen years until his death in 1645. Ironically, of all those involved in the drama which had literally threatened the throne, Sir Thomas Overbury was the only one to obtain at least posthumous fame when his poem called *The Wife* was published and due to trial's publicity, became one of the best-sellers of the age.

CHAPTER 7
The Lure of Spanish Gold

King James was diverted from his anxiety over his involvement in the tragic fate of Sir Thomas Overbury, by consultation with King Philip of Spain. Negotiations for the marriage of his heir, Prince Charles, the Prince of Wales, to the little Princess Christina, daughter of the King of France, begun in 1613, had lasted for three years. But, in 1616, James had a change of mind. A charismatic Spanish ambassador, Sarmiento de Acuna, Diego, (later Count Gondomar) had arrived in London just as arrangements for the French marriage were being put in hand.

Sarmiento was a man after James' own heart. Quick-witted and amusing, he went hunting with the King and according to the Venetian ambassador, 'vied with him in putting his hands in the blood of bucks and stags,'–James being the man who almost fainted at the very sight of human gore–'doing cheerfully everything that his Majesty does and in this way chiefly he has acquired his favour.'[105]

Forthwith, during many conversations, Sarmiento contrived to convince the King of the wealth and power of Spain, until the King finally admitted that Philip, 'had many kingdoms and more subjects beyond comparison than did he.' But nonetheless the ambassador insisted that the King of Spain was deeply interested in winning his friendship. Philip longed, so Sarmiento assured him, to forget old quarrels and to live with 'the British Solomon' as a brother, as James, greatly flattered, was only too pleased to hear. Once allied to Spain, Sarmiento assured him, 'his enemies would yield in abashed submission, or fade away with little shrieks of despair.' The English Roman Catholics would become his greatest supporters. His fears of assassination would vanish forthwith.

Then following the dissolution of Parliament in 1614, King James, acutely aware of the parlous state of his treasury, began to envisage an alignment with Spain as the answer to all his monetary problems and it was at this point that Sarmiento suggested a Spanish marriage for Prince Charles. King Philip consulted the Pope who was strongly against the match, but despite this the Spanish government, on their English ambassador's advice, prepared articles to start negotiations.

Six months went by and the marriage proposals lay in abeyance while James was pre-occupied with the militant Catholics in Ireland. His fears for his own safety intensified when John Owen, a fanatical English Catholic, publicly declared that 'the King, being excommunicated by the Pope, might be lawfully deposed and killed.' Paranoid with terror, James slept for some time behind a barricade of empty beds and when venturing outside drove in his carriage at full tilt surrounded by running footmen.

Sometime towards the end of January 1616, he summoned Sarmiento to his presence, asking him to resume the marriage discussions with Spain. But King Philip was dilatory and the King, growing impatient, conceived the idea of forcing him into activity by challenging his appropriation of settlements in the southern part of North America.

And who better to do so than the man who, on a charge of treason and involvement in the Main Plot, as far back as 1603, had been held prisoner in the Tower for over ten years–Sir Walter Raleigh.

Raleigh, Queen Elizabeth's hero of the Spanish Armada, was now, by the standards of the day, an old man of sixty-two. During his long years of captivity he had constantly dreamed of El Dorado, the golden city of Manoa which, according to Indian folklore, lay at the head of the Caroni, the second largest river in Venezuela, which, after its confluence with the Orinoco, runs through the same basin to the sea.

Although it was now almost twenty years since Raleigh had visited the region, he remained convinced that, as the result of his voyage there, it still belonged legally to England. That this was much disputed, he already knew. In 1596 he had sent an expedition there under Laurence Keymis, his companion and fellow explorer on previous voyages. Keymis, as captain of the

Darling, had continued to explore the Guiana coast and Essequibo River, returning with glowing accounts of the country he had visited and assuring Raleigh that it would greatly benefit the then-reigning Queen Elizabeth to take possession of it. But he did also warn him that the Spanish had established ownership of the Orinoco and the Caroni rivers and had built a settlement called San Thomée near to the place of their confluence.

King James longed passionately for wealth. Just as when as a young man the Ruthvens had lured him to the house in Perth, promising fabled gold, he now believed in Raleigh's assertion that gold mines lay close to the Orinoco and that if anyone could find it he could.

Thus, in the summer of 1617, Raleigh sailed for Venezuela. He went, having given a solemn pledge to the King, that he would go only to the mines and that neither would he either rob or in any way attack any subject of Spain. The Spanish ambassador protested loudly but James assured him that he would send Raleigh, bound hand and foot to Spain, if he broke his word regarding his compatriots. Furthermore, if he came back bringing stolen Spanish gold, James would restore it to Philip and send Raleigh to be hanged in Madrid.

The voyage was catastrophic from its start. The ships were first battered by a hurricane and then lay motionless in the doldrums while fever ravaged the crews. Raleigh himself was so ill, that when he finally reached the mouth of the Orinoco he could not go ashore. Unwillingly, he surrendered command to Laurence Keymis, who landed close to San Thomée to be fired on by Spanish marksmen. Infuriated, the English stormed the settlement, young Walter, Raleigh's eldest son, being killed by a bullet as he ran towards the town.

The attack was at least successful. Keymis held the position for a month until, with his men almost starving and with no discovery of gold, he was forced to retire back to the ships, where, having told Raleigh of his failure, he killed himself from shame.

Raleigh himself was devastated, writing to his wife of Walter's death, he told her 'God knows I never knew what sorrow meant till now,' before, with no apparent alternative, he sadly set sail for home.

His return was predictably foreseen. Raleigh was made the scapegoat for what was, from the first, a badly-conceived plan to invade a settlement known to be in Spanish hands. Coming ashore at Plymouth on 21 June 1618, he was quickly arrested and sent once more to the Tower.

King James, desperate to remain on good terms with Spain, dispatched his apologies to King Philip through the latter's ambassador, now Count Gondomar. 'His Majesty is very disposed and determined against Raleigh and will join with the King of Spain in ruining him,' he wrote. Gondomar then, in an interview with James, told him flatly that if he had the power he would punish Raleigh himself. The King, distracted, threw his hat on the floor and clutched his hair shouting that, "till God forsook him, he would not punish a man unheard."

He then appointed a commission of councillors, who included both Sir Francis Bacon and Sir Edward Coke, to hear Raleigh's case. They concluded that he had been plotting with France, that the story of the gold was invention and that Raleigh's prime target had been the plundering of the Spanish in America, offences meriting execution.

Raleigh died as bravely as he had lived, his last words to a wavering executioner being, "strike man, strike!" In killing him James placated the Spaniards but in England people accused him of creating a national disgrace.

After fourteen years as King of Great Britain, as he proudly called himself, King James returned only once, in 1617, to Scotland, land of his birth.

Once there he hunted happily in his old haunts round Falkland Palace and in Perthshire. More importantly, having already introduced King James's Bible, still in use in some churches today, in 1618 he imposed the Five Articles of Perth curtailing the ultra-Presbyterianism of the Scottish Kirk. Henceforth, Scots must kneel at communion and the celebration of Christian festivals, in accordance with the Anglican faith, a ruling which, unforeseen by James, was to be the cause of such resentment in the time of his son Charles I.

James returned from Scotland to face a crisis. Five years earlier, his beautiful daughter Elizabeth had married Frederick,

Elector of the Palatinate, a region in south-west Germany. Now came word that the aged and childless Matthias, the Holy Roman Emperor, King of Hungary and Croatia and King of Bohemia since 1611, had determined to make his cousin Ferdinand of Styria his heir. The largely Protestant Bohemian nobles had risen in revolt and in May 1618 had invaded the palace in Prague, capital city of Bohemia to seize the Emperor's regents and throw them out of the windows before taking possession of the country. Now Protestants and Catholics in Germany were on the verge of what would develop into the Thirty years War.

Following their occupation of Bohemia, the German Calvinists, their leader James' son-in-law, Frederick Elector of the Palatinate, saw a chance to destroy the rule of the Austrian Habsburgs forever.

King James found himself in a dilemma. King Philip of Spain, his greatest protagonist in Europe, whose daughter he hoped his son Prince Charles would marry, was bound to the Holy Roman Emperor both through relationship and interest. The Elector Frederick begged his father-in-law, to send an army to help him but in July came a request from King Philip that James should act as mediator between the new Emperor Ferdinand (Matthias had died in March) and the Bohemians.

But hardly had this happened before, in August 1619 the Bohemians deposed Ferdinand as their King and elected Frederick of the Palatinate in his place. Frederick, faced with the enormity of the situation, prevaricated, but then made the ill-fated decision to accept and together with Elizabeth, travelled to Prague in October.

King James was greatly distressed, detesting war for any cause whatever, he was convinced that Frederick, in accepting the kingship of Bohemia had become the supporter of rebels. By sending an army to help him, his reputation as the peacemaker of Christendom would be destroyed. Also, inevitably, it must put an end to Prince Charles' marriage to the Infanta, Maria Anna, on which he had set such store. Convinced that the Spanish would incite the English Catholics to rebellion, James believed his life would be constantly threatened as before. According to the Venetian ambassador, the King sincerely believed that 'he could not keep peace or even remain alive' except by forming an alliance with Spain.

To the Spanish ambassador, Count Gondomar, recently returned from Spain, he swept off his hat and mopping his brow declared that, 'as a king, as a gentleman, as a Christian, and as an honest man, I have no wish to marry my son to anyone except your master's daughter, and that I desire no alliance but that with Spain.' Then, in reply to the burning question, as to whether the Emperor Ferdinand would attack Spain, Gondomer asked him outright if anyone had taken London what would he do? To which the King, at a loss for an answer, said that he hoped God would arrange matters for the best.[106]

But the Almighty failed to intervene. In August 1620 a Spanish army from the Netherlands invaded the Palatinate while, at the same time, the Emperor Ferdinand's forces advanced into Prague.

James was incandescent with rage. Gondomar had deceived him. He would never trust a Spaniard again! And forthwith he declared to the Council that he would relieve the Palatinate himself.

But, above all things, he shrank from war and convinced that Philip would keep to his promise to restore the Palatinate, once Frederick had renounced all claims to Bohemia, he sent John Digby (later the Earl of Bristol) to Vienna to offer Frederick's renunciation of Bohemia as a basis for making peace. Digby did achieve a temporary truce, which was broken almost as soon as it was made. Maximilian, the Emperor of Bavaria, invaded the Upper Palatinate while the Spanish army conquered the Lower part of the country. Digby came back to England in October saying Frederick's cause was lost unless James would send an army to save him.

A Parliament called in November, agreed that money should be sent to Frederick, while military action was prepared. But the Commons then produced a petition, demanding not only the enforcement of the anti-Catholic laws in England, but a war against Spain and that Prince Charles should marry a Protestant.

James in a fury at such insubordination, wrote to the Speaker, commanding that henceforth no member of parliament should meddle with his government, nor with deep mysteries of the State, nor, 'deal with our dearest son's match with the daughter of Spain, nor touch the honour of that King.' On top of this he dictated, that in no way would he receive the Commons petition, unless in a greatly modified form.

A second request was then taken to the King at Newmarket by twelve of the Commons. James received them graciously and told them that as long as they kept within the limits of their duty, he would uphold their lawful liberties, but they must not go beyond their rights. The Commons then drew up a protest. They would quarrel with the King no longer but would set down a statement of their entitlements, including that every member had freedom of speech without the fear of arrest.

Greatly affronted by such defiance, King James was then told by Count Gondomar that Spain could not negotiate while such a parliament remained. Undecided he prevaricated until, at the end of December, on the advice of both his son and Buckingham, he resolved to dissolve Parliament. Gondomar, triumphant, called it the best thing that had happened during the last hundred years, but it meant that, without the enforcement of his government to raise an army, James could not send help to his daughter and her husband, in the Palatinate. The result was foreseeable. On 8 November 1620, Frederick, so briefly the King of Bohemia, was defeated at the Battle of White Mountain, by a large Imperial army.

With his wife, the lovely Elizabeth, known henceforward for the length of her husband's reign as the Winter Queen, Frederick fled the Palatinate, first to Germany and then, at the invitation of the Prince of Orange, to live in exile at the Hague.

James, deeply depressed and feeling himself partly responsible for what had happened, rode off to Newmarket, unknowingly at the risk of his life. But this time it was not the assassin who awaited him, but a river covered in ice. He had just passed his house of Theobolds in Essex when, on the hard rutted ground, his horse stumbled sending him head-first, into the New River, plunging through thin ice. Sir Richard Young, fortunately very close behind, saw nothing but the royal boots sticking out above the ice. Leaping off his horse he waded into the freezing water and seizing them pulled the King out. Soaked and choking, James did manage to ride back the short way to Theobolds, where, put into a warm bed, he thawed out none the worse.

The King, by the mercy of Providence, had once again cheated death.

CHAPTER 8

'But as the Sun Sets, Only for to Rise' (Epitaph for Queen Anne by King James)

James was now a widower, his queen, Anne of Denmark, from whom he had been estranged for the last ten years of her life, having died shortly after his return to England, in 1619. His affection for her, if it ever existed–the only thing they ever shared apparently was a love of hunting–was soon eclipsed by his adoration of his favourite, George Villiers, whom he created, first Earl, then Marquis and finally Duke of Buckingham in 1618. The King, who nicknamed him Steenie, after St Stephen who had the face of an angel, famously declared that, 'You may be sure that I love the Earl of Buckingham more than anyone else, and more than you who are here assembled. I wish to speak in my own behalf and not to have it thought to be a defect, for Jesus Christ did the same, and therefore I cannot be blamed. Christ had John, and I have George.'

The latter part of the reign of James VI and I is now largely remembered for his inauguration of colonisation both in Ireland and North America. From his first arrival in England James had begun his well-organised system of peopling the north-west of Ireland where most of the land had been forfeited by the rebellion in which the Earls of Tyrone and Tyreconnell and the great northern chief Sir Cahir O'Dogharty, had taken so great a part, reducing the land to waste. Colonists from both England and Scotland were given grants of land to encourage them to settle and to establish the Anglican and Presbyterian churches in a hitherto Catholic dominated country.

Foremost amongst those who seized the chance to obtain estates in Ireland was George Villiers, who by 1616 had a strong hold over the King. James agreed to his suggestion that Villier's close friend, Sir Oliver St John, be made Lord Deputy of Ireland. Thence, in 1618, Villiers acquired control of the Irish Customs Farm, after which he dominated Irish interests at court particularly in the sale of Irish titles and honours and at the same time by exploiting the plantation lobby in Dublin, gaining Irish estates both for himself, his relations and friends and finally, in 1622, organising the Irish Court of Wards.

Buckingham, as Villiers now was, had felt some trepidation when, in the previous year of 1621, Parliament had begun an investigation into abuses of monopolies both in England and later in Ireland. While making a bold show of support, as the King decided to send a commission of enquiry to Ireland, he secretly dreaded the outcome. However, knowing that James had assured the Spanish ambassador, Count Gondomar, that the parliament would be forbidden to interfere with the much vaunted Spanish alliance, involving the marriage of the Infanta with his son, he contrived to engineer the Parliament's dissolution and subsequently a diminution of the Irish commission in 1622.

Previous to this, in 1607, three years after the Treaty of London had established peace with Spain, allowing Englishmen access to the new world of North America. The first settlement there had been established in Jamestown, Virginia on the east side of the continent. One of James' vagaries however, was his detestation of tobacco and in 1616, told that they were planting it, he had ordered the colonists to plant hemp, fruit and vineyards and mulberry trees for raising silkworms in its place. Silkworms, already sent to Virginia, had unfortunately been lost at sea.

The King had formed a close friendship with Sir William Alexander, the Scottish courtier-poet who came from Menstrie near Stirling, who had helped him with the metrical version known as 'The Psalms of King David,' which, translated by James, was later to be published under the authority of Charles I. Beginning his career as tutor to the Earl of Argyll, Alexander had then become a Gentleman Usher to Prince Charles. James, recognizing a kindred spirit, made Alexander firstly master of Requests for Scotland, effectively his private secretary and then, in 1615, a member of the Scottish Privy Council.

Determined that Scotland should share in the booming growth of plantations, Alexander soon won King James' support to the idea. In 1621 he granted him, under the Scottish Crown, all the territories lying between New England and Newfoundland. Planned to be called New Scotland, the charter being in Latin, resulted in Nova Scotia. Then the King, deciding to make it a work of his own, created an order of baronets of Nova Scotia, open to all Scots who would produce the money to develop the new colony.

Nonetheless it was Sir William Alexander whose name was to be for ever associated with the foundation of the Scottish colonisation of Port Royal, Nova Scotia and Long Island, New York.

But if gaining land was the prime object of the Scottish settlers, it was in search of religious freedom, that in 1620, the Puritan Pilgrim Fathers sailed across the Atlantic to settle in Plymouth Massachusetts.

Scottish settlement in India was less successful. Having confirmed the East India Company's monopoly, James then allowed an adventurer called Sir Edward Michaelbourne to sail as a trader to the east where he attacked and plundered native shipping to the Company's great embarrassment. Worse was to come in 1622, when the King, driven by his familiar avarice for money–so nearly the cause of his death in the Gowrie's house in Perth so many years ago–committed one of the most despicable acts of his reign.

The East India Company had successfully driven the Portuguese from Ormuz and set up an English factory on this very strategic site. On news of this happening, James insisted, that although the royal navy had not been involved, the Company must give both himself and the Lord Admiral, Buckingham, £10,000 each of the booty for themselves.

It was in the autumn of 1622 that Buckingham suggested to King James, that once the arrangements for the Spanish marriage were complete, nothing could be more fitting than that he, as the Lord Admiral, should travel out to Spain to escort the Infanta Maria Anna back to England. Prince Charles could go with him in disguise. The King demurred at the idea, unwilling to commit himself until all was signed and sealed. But his hand was forced in the following February when Charles and Buckingham announced that they wished to depart at once. They would ride across France disguised, and without bothering to get a passport from the French authorities, force through the final negotiations and return with the Spanish bride.

James initially agreed but then had second thoughts. Sending for Sir Francis Cottington, a former ambassador to Spain who was now secretary to Prince Charles, he poured out his fears. 'Here are Baby Charles and Steenie who have a great mind to go by post to Spain to fetch home the Infanta, and will have but two more in their company, and have chosen you for one. What think you of the journey?'[107]

Cottington was horrified. Such an adventure would certainly undo all that had been so far decided. The Spanish would be bound to raise their terms. On hearing this, the King threw himself onto his bed, sobbing and crying, "I am undone. I shall lose Baby Charles," before, calming down, he eventually capitulated to the pressure of the two young men. Consequently, on 17 February 1523, Buckingham and Charles, calling themselves Tom and Jack Smith, rode in disguise to Dover where they found a ship to take them to Boulogne. From there they went boldly to Paris, where they stayed for two days, before heading south through a pass in the Pyrenees mountains to reach Madrid on 7 March.

At home in England, where the news of their arrival at the Spanish capital was soon known, King James was far more concerned about the health and safety of the travellers than by any affairs of state. 'God bless you both, my sweet boys,' he wrote to them, 'and send you, after a successful journey, a joyful return into the arms of your dear dad. I wear Steenie's picture in a blue ribbon under my wash-coat next my heart.'[108] Paranoid about Charles's health, he told Charles not to tilt under the hot Spanish sun and instead suggested that he and Buckingham should keep themselves fit by dancing, "though ye should whistle and sing to one another, like Jack and Tom, for fault of better music."

Subsequently, in 1623, King James signed the articles of marriage between his son Prince Charles and King Philip's daughter, the Infanta Maria Anna of Spain. In addition to this, by means of a private letter, he promised to relieve the English

Catholics from the laws prohibiting their religion on condition they did not ignite public scandal.[109]

By this time two ships had been prepared to carry Charles' servants to Spain. With them, they would take the Prince and Buckingham's robes and insignia of the Garter together with some carefully chosen jewels, James insisting that they must dine in them to impress the Spaniards on 23 April, St George's Day.

James, now greatly excited, believing his long-cherished prospect of his son's Spanish marriage to be all but achieved, spared himself no expense in preparing to receive the Infanta. No less than eight great ships and two pinnaces were to sail to Spain to bring back Charles and the bride for whom a magnificent cabin–fit for a goddess–was specially made. Likewise a wing of St James' Palace was enlarged for her apartments, an oratory added and the whole place redecorated in her honour.

"God knows my coffers are drained," James lamented, as suffering from acute arthritis, he lay on his bed in much pain.

But it proved to be all in vain. Charles was well-received in Spain but not allowed to meet, or even speak to, or see the Infanta. One reason for this appears to have been that the Pope's permission for the marriage had not yet arrived. Buckingham, told that the holdup was due to the King of England's refusal to grant full liberty of worship to Roman Catholics, replied that this was impossible, whereupon King Philip secretly advised the Pope to refuse the dispensation. The Pope, however, intent upon advancing Catholicism, thought otherwise. He did allow the dispensation, but only on the condition that the Infanta must control the education of her children until they were twelve and that English Catholics, instead of taking the oath of allegiance, might substitute an oath drawn up by himself for the servants of the Infanta to which James must obtain the consent of both his Council and his Parliament.

Buckingham was furious but Charles said that he was willing to accept the Pope's decree. But a junta of Spanish theologians then announced that King James must make a public declaration abolishing the laws against Catholics and swear they would never be reimposed. Then, finally, they insisted that following her marriage, the Infanta must stay in Spain for another year.

In England, the King grew more and more desperate to know what was happening in Spain. Afraid that his precious 'Baby Charles' and his equally adored Buckingham might be taken prisoner, he ordered them to abandon the marriage treaty and come home. "I care for match nor nothing, so I may once have you in my arms again…and let me hear from you quickly, with all speed, as you love my life, and so God send you a happy and joyful meeting in the arms of your dear dad."[110]

On reading his father's letter, Charles first said he would return to England and then, suddenly accepting the Spanish terms, signed the marriage treaty on St James's Day, 25 July. King James, told of this happening, summoned his councillors, weeping as he told them that his son would remain a prisoner in Spain if he refused to agree to their terms. "All the devils in hell and all the Puritans in England could now not stop the match. Since it can be no better, I must be content."[111]

Impatiently, he waited to hear that the wedding had taken place, that the Infanta with her much needed dowry of £600,000 was already on her way to England. But Charles had suddenly changed his mind. Disillusioned by the discovery that the promised Spanish aid for the Palatinate was a deception and possibly by having seen the Infanta in the theatre and found her less beautiful than he had imagined, he announced he was going back to England. The Spaniards, in fact, by now wanted to get rid of him, and in September, on his threatening to leave, he was virtually pushed out from Madrid.

Together with Buckingham, he landed at Portsmouth on 5 October 1623 and went at once to the King to be received with rapturous delight.

King James's state of euphoria, however, lasted only a few days. His favourite Buckingham and his son Charles were now openly demanding war with Spain. James was horrified. Abhorring war as he did, he still believed King Philip to be his best support in Europe, and when he heard that his son and Buckingham were lambasting pro-Spanish ministers and allying themselves with the anti-Spanish faction in parliament, he told them bluntly they were fools.

But now, no one listened to James. Ill and greatly confused, he found that power was being wrested from his hands. Prince Charles and Buckingham were in fact ruling the country, declaring that the Prince's marriage to the Infanta should be postponed until her father kept to his former word of restoring the Elector Frederick to the Palatinate. James was kept virtually a prisoner. Housebound by arthritis amongst his many other ills, he moaned that he was a poor old man who had once known how to rule but who had now lost his skill.[112]

The last word on the Spanish Match was the vote of the Privy Council, in January 1624, to reject the Spanish terms. The Prince and Buckingham then demanded a summoning of Parliament, to which, James, knowing it would be strongly anti-Spanish, most unwillingly agreed to it being convened in the following month of February.

The Spanish treaties abandoned. Charles and Buckingham, through the following months, persisted in planning a grand alliance against Spain.

But the truth was that James, still struggling to save the Palatinate, could simply not afford another war. Britain was in the throes of a great depression. Trade was falling dramatically. The King's chief financial advisor, Sir Lionel Cranfield, whom he had ennobled as the Earl of Middlesex, suggested cuts in the pension bill over which the King had been consistently extravagant. But Cranfield himself, who had made many enemies including Buckingham, in May 1624, was impeached by the government, 'for bribery, extortion, oppression, wrong and deceits.'[113]

Now it was France that was courted with the assent of the King. A new marriage treaty was engendered between Charles and the Princess Henrietta Maria, sister of King Louis XIII. Difficulty arose, however, because on the insistence of the all-powerful Cardinal Richelieu, as in the previous Spanish engagement, secret clauses to liberate the English Catholics were included in the proposed marriage settlement. The King had promised the House of Commons that no future marriage treaties would include concessions to the English Catholics, but Buckingham bullied him into breaking his word.

James did then send a British army to Holland to try to rescue the Palatinate for his daughter Elizabeth and her husband, King Frederick of Bohemia, now living as exiles in the Hague. Buckingham led an expedition to La Rochelle, aimed at relieving the Huguenots, which ended in disaster. James then refused to let his army go to the relief of the Dutch town of Breda, under siege from the Spanish, despite urgent pleas from King Louis.

King James struggled on, by now sometimes confused in his mind and plainly unwell. On 5 March 1625, at Theobolds, the country house twelve miles north of London which he had persuaded Robert Cecil, Lord Salisbury, to exchange for Hatfield House, probably as the result of hunting when suffering from a cold, he developed influenza. A few days later, he collapsed, it is thought from a stroke, which robbed him of his speech. The doctors could do nothing, and Buckingham and his mother, in desperation, tried some of the old wife's recipes for relieving congestion on the chest. One concoction, a mixture of black plaster and powder which he took by mouth, was believed by Sir Anthony Weldon amongst others to be poison, the suspicion lingering for nearly quarter of a century until at the trial of his son, Charles I, that unfortunate monarch was even accused of colluding with Buckingham to administer poison to his father, thereby causing his death.

So died James VI of Scotland and I of Britain, survivor of all the attempts to kill him that began when he was still in his mother's womb. Kidnappers had failed to seize him, the steel of Alexander Ruthven's sword had actually lain across his throat, in the attempt of assassination in the Guthrie's house in Perth, which James himself had foiled. Then, later, in England, the attempt of Catesby and his fellow conspirators to blow him apart with gunpowder had backfired. No more fortunate had been the alchemists, those faceless men who had supplied poison to kill Thomas Overbury at Frances Somerset's bequest. James, in this case, had escaped involvement in a crime which, had anything been proved against him, might have led to his degradation and even dethronement, much to his enemy's gain.

But he had survived them all: the plots to either kill or usurp him in so many different ways. King James, in the forty years for which, since the age of fourteen he had reigned, had resembled a wise pilot, steering both the countries of his kingdom through a narrow channel of safety between the rocks and pitfalls of threatened European wars. He was in fact the great dissembler, who earned himself the name of peacemaker, in his dealings with politicians both within his own shores and abroad. Diffident he might be, as in his attempts to save the throne of his son-in-law,

Frederick of the Palatinate, but behind his apparent indecision lay the acute perception of a man who could foresee the ultimate consequences of involvement in the quarrels of foreign powers.

James was essentially a British king, a man whose own tastes were simple despite the accusations of extravagance made largely by those envious of the favourites on whom he lavished so much money and land. A family man who loved his children and to some extent his wife, he accepted responsibility as inevitable, convinced as he was, by both education and belief, of the divine right of kings.

Most outstanding of his achievements was the establishment of peace between the two countries over which he ruled. Scotland, in particular, had been brought to near ruination by the wars, fought both by his grandfather James V and his great-grandfather James IV, against England largely at the instigation of promised support by the kings of France. In Scotland, in particular, the years of peace between the two countries, saw a rise in the standard of living of people, hitherto accustomed to existing on a knife-edge of starvation and poverty caused by fighting, not only with England, but to a lesser degree amongst themselves. True more than a hundred years were to pass before legislation, following the Jacobite Rising of 1745, was to banish the power of hereditary jurisdiction, so much the cause of clan warfare between rival chiefs. But it was King James VI, that inauspicious, over-emotional monarch, ever seeking the love denied to him in his childhood, for which he so greatly craved, the ungainly, rather pathetic figure that contemporary reports portray, who laid the foundation of the united country, that some two hundred years later, would be the most powerful in the world.

INDEX

D

E

REFERENCES

[1] A.P.S.ii 411-13, 425-6.

[2] Strickland Agnes, *Lives of the Queens of Scotland and English Princesses*. Vol.ii. p.201.

[3] Lindsay of Pitscottie, Robert, Chronicles of Scotland, vol.2. Edinburgh (1814), 424-429.

[4] Coventry, Martin. The Castles of Scotland, 2nd Ed. P.150.

[5] Smith, John Guthrie (1886). *The Parish of Strathblane,* The University Press Glasgow, p.87

[6] Melville, Sir James of Halhill. *Memoirs of.* Pub. The Folio Society London 1969. P. 103.

[7] Strickland. p.363.

[8] Fraser, Antonia. *Mary Queen of Scots*.p.237.

[9] Ibid.

[10] Bingham, Caroline, *Darnley*, p.164.

[11] Mahon, Major-General, R.H.*A Study of the Lennox Narrative,* p.124.

[12] Fraser. p.376.

[13] Melville, Sir James of Hallhill, Memoirs of. Pub. The Folio Society London 1969. p.64.

[14] ibid. pp.65-6.

[15] Ibid. p.66.

[16] Ibid. p.67.

[17] Ibid. p.103.

[18] Melville, Sir James, 'The Memoirs of Sir James Melville of Hallhill.* Folio Edition London, 1969. pp.103-4.

[19] Ibid.p.104.

[20] Lord Herries, Memoirs, p.133.

[21] Fraser, Antonia, *Mary Queen of Scots*, p.498.

[22] Bingham. p. 42.

[23] Thomson, Thomas (1833) A diurnal of remarkable occurrents that have passed within the country of Scotland (in Scots). Bannatyne Club. p.173.

[24] *The Records of the Parliament of Scotland to 1707.* Ed. Brown. K.M. University of St Andrews. pp.1570/10/1.

[25] Lord Herries, *Memoirs*, p.133.

[26] *Accounts of the Treasurer of Scotland.* Vol.12. HMSO. 1970. P.365.

[27] Records of the Parliaments of Scotland to 1707. University of St Andrews.pp.1571/8/15.

[28] *Diurnal of Remarkable Occurrents* (1513-1475) ed. Thomson, Bannatyne and Maitland Clubs, 1833.p.242.

[29] Ibid. p. 91.

[30] Ibid. p.96.

[31] *Register of the Privy Council of Scotland*, Vol.2, pp.663-4.

[32] Melville, p.105.

[33] Calderwood, David. History of the Kirk of Scotland, Vol.iii, pp.442-3.

[34] Ibid. pp.457-8.

[35] The correspondence of Robert Bowes, of Aske, esq, the ambassador of Queen Elizabeth to the court of Scotland. Surtees Society. 1842. pp.105–9.

[36] Wilson, D.H. *King James VI & I.* p.39.

[37] Diary of James Melville, (Woodrow Soc.) pp. 119-20.

[38] Ibid, p.636.

[39] Melville.p.108.

[40] Wilson, D.N. King James VI & I.pp.42-3.

[41] Smith, John Guthrie, *The Parish of Strathblane*. pp.116–18.

[42] Ibid. p.110.

[43] Calderwood, vol.iv. p.399.

[44] Melville. p.124.

[45] Edmonstone, Sir Archibald of Duntreath. Genealogical Account of the Family of Edmonstone of Duntreath. p.40.

[46] Ibid.p.41.

[47] Ibid.

[48] Hume of Godscroft, *History of the Douglasses*, folio, p.391.

[49] Cal. S. P. Scot., viii 43-5.

[50] Wilson. p.56.

[51] Donaldson, Gordon, ed., *Register of the Privy Seal of Scotland*, vol.8. p.413 no.2369.

[52] Melville. p.124.

[53] Sir Archibald Edmonstone of Duntreath, *Genealogical Account of the Family of Edmonstone of Duntreath*. Edinburgh, privately printed, MDCCCLXXV, pp.40-3.

[54] Wilson, D.H.p.72.

[55] Wilson. D.H. p. 97.

[56] Calendar State Papers Scottish, 1589-1583, 257, 281-308, 315, 325, 330, 456–7.

[57] Ibid. pp.79-84.

[58] National Archives of Scotland GD224/890/21.

[59] Goodare. J, 'The Scottish witchcraft act'' Church History, 74 (2005), 39-67.

[60] *Calendar State Papers Domestic 1691-94*, London (1867), pp.368-9.

[61] Gregory Donald, *History of the Western Highlands and Isles of Scotland* pp.250–1.

[62] National Library of Scotland, Adv. Mss.35.4.2

[63] H.M.C., *Manuscripts of the Marquis of Salisbury at Hatfield House*, BVol.10. (1904).pp.40,61,72,440: CSP Scotland,Vol.13 part 1 (1969).pp.257,260,263.

[64] Wilson, D.H. p.123.

[65] Ibid. p.119.

[66] MacGregor, Miss A.G.M. History of the Clan Gregor, Vol 1. P.153.

[67] Ramsay, Dr. A.A.W. The Arrow of Glenlyon. pp.114–15.

[68] Notes from the Exchequer Rolls, in Haddington's M.S. Collections, Advocates Library.

[69] Gregory, pp.287–8.

[70] R.P.C, (records of the Privy Council) vol.vi, p.216.

[71] Ibid. pp.402–4.

[72] Ramsay. A, A. W. The Arrow of Glenlyon, pp.146-7.

[73] Acts of Parliament Scotland .iv. 212-13.

[74] Fraser. p.80.

[75] Ibid. p.86.

[76] R.P.C. (Records of Privy Council) Vol.vii, p.749.

[77] Wilson. p.163.

[78] Ibid. p.180.

[79] Ibid. pp.164-5.

[80] Gristwood, S. *Arbella, England's Lost Queen*. P217.

[81] Ibid p.205.

[82] Ibid. pp. 48-50.

[83] Brydges, Sir Egerton, Restiituta or, Titles, extracts, and characters of old books in English Literature.

[84] Wormald, Jenny 'Gunpowder, Treason and Scots' pp.141-168.

[85] Gardiner, Samuel Rawson, Gerard John, *What Gunpowder Plot was*. Pub. Longmans 1897. P.59.

[86] Fraser, pp.90-5.

[87] Gerard. John (1871) *The condition of Catholics under James I: Father Gerard's narrative of the Gunpowder Plot*, p.57.

[88] Haynes, Alan The Gunpowder Plot: Faith in Rebellion, pp.44–5.

[89] Nicholls Mark, 'Percy, Thomas, (1560-1605) *Oxford Dictionary of National Biography*.

[90] Fraser, p.84.

[91] Fraser, pp.47–50.

[92] Haynes A, *The Gunpowder Plot*, p.49.

[93] Ibid. p.50.

[94] Fraser. p.41.

[95] Haynes, A. *The Enduring Memory of the Gunpowder Plot*, BBC,co,uk

[96] Haynes, A. *The Gunpowder Plot*. p.76.

[97] Ibid.

[98] Cobbett, William. *A History of the Protestant Reformation in England and Ireland*, Simpkin, Marshall and Company. p.229.

[99] Fraser, pp. 215-16, 228-9.

[100] Ibid. p.100.

101 *Somer's Tracts*, Printed for T. Cadell and W. Davies (etc.). 1809-1815

13 v.; [This collection can also be found within British Culture: Series One].Vol.xi, p.113.

102 Wikipedia.

103 Sir Henry Wotton. Lie and Letter of. Vol.I pp.113-25.

104 Goodman, Godfrey, Bishop of Gloucester, quoted in Gregg, Pauline, (1884) King Charles I. Berkeley. C.A. University of California Press. P49.

105 Wilson, D.H. King James VI& I.

106 Ibid. p.414.

107 Wilson. pp.431–2.

108 Ibid. p.433.

109 Fraser, p.202.

110 Ibid.p.204.

111 Wilson.p.439.

112 Ibid. p.441.

113 Fraser. p.208.

CPSIA information can be obtained
at www.ICGtesting.com
Printed in the USA
BVHW051354080623
665608BV00016B/1131

9 781788 782074